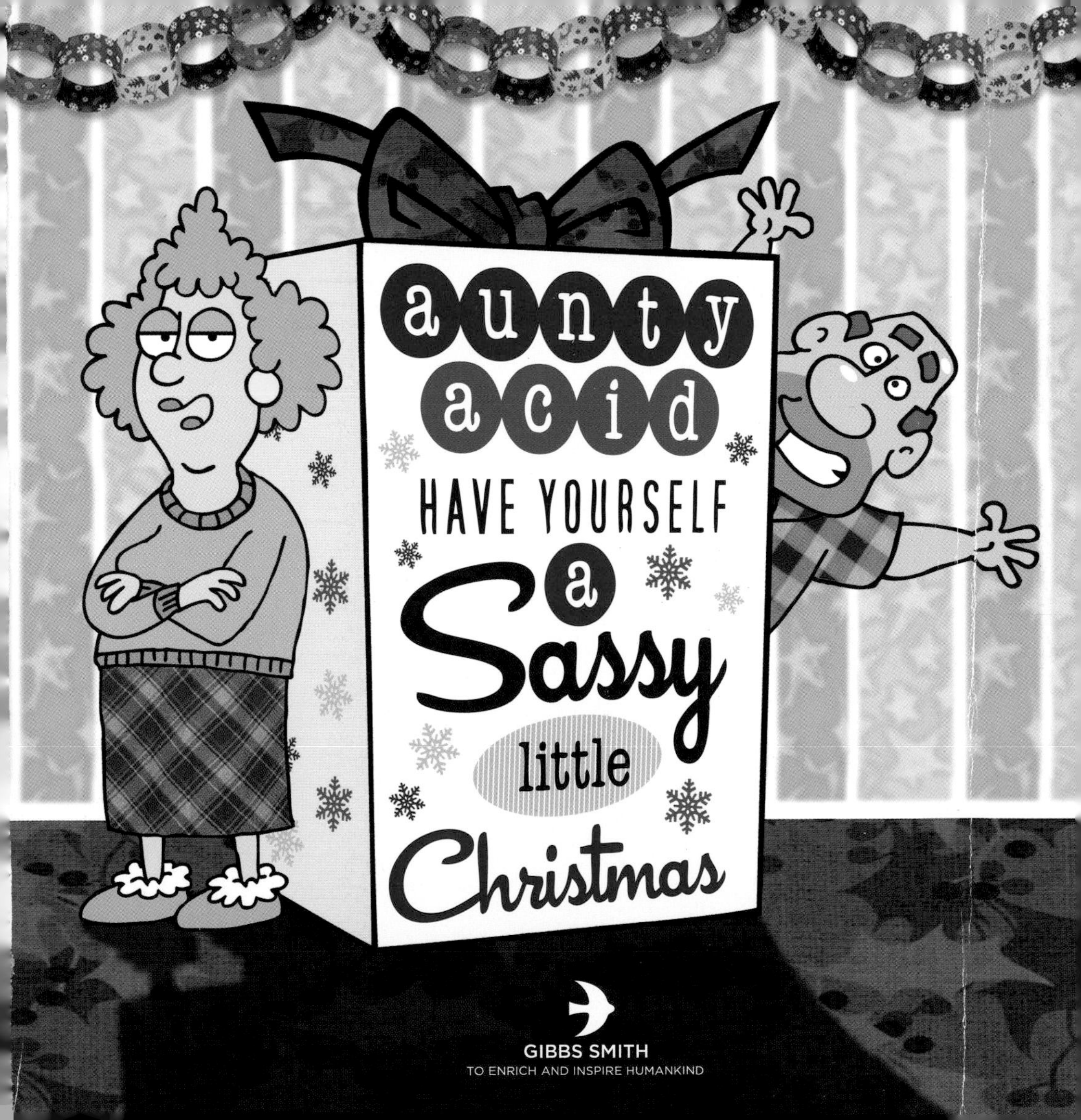
aunty acid
HAVE YOURSELF
a Sassy
little
Christmas
GIBBS SMITH
TO ENRICH AND INSPIRE HUMANKIND

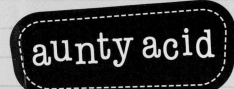

aunty acid letter to Santa

Dear Santa,

I hope I'm not on your **naughty** **list** this year....

I reckon I've been very good, considering the number of freakin' **idiots** I've been surrounded by.

I've hardly made anybody cry, and even Walt agrees that he **deserved** to be locked in the basement that day.

As for what I'll be putting on my Christmas list this year...

all I want is peace on earth.

...Seriously, can't you make everybody please be quiet for just one freakin' day?

Thankfully my mother-in-law has decided to stay at home this year, so it turns out Christmas miracles do happen!

I have to go now; my festive shaped cookies are burning in the oven. Who says you can't burn 2,000 calories in under 30 minutes, huh?

Which reminds me...if you could leave me a new birthday suit this year that would be great. The one I have is old, wrinkled and starting to sag.

Sincerely,

Aunty Annie Acid
45 No Freakin' Way
Bite Me Avenue
Crazy Town
CT-66643

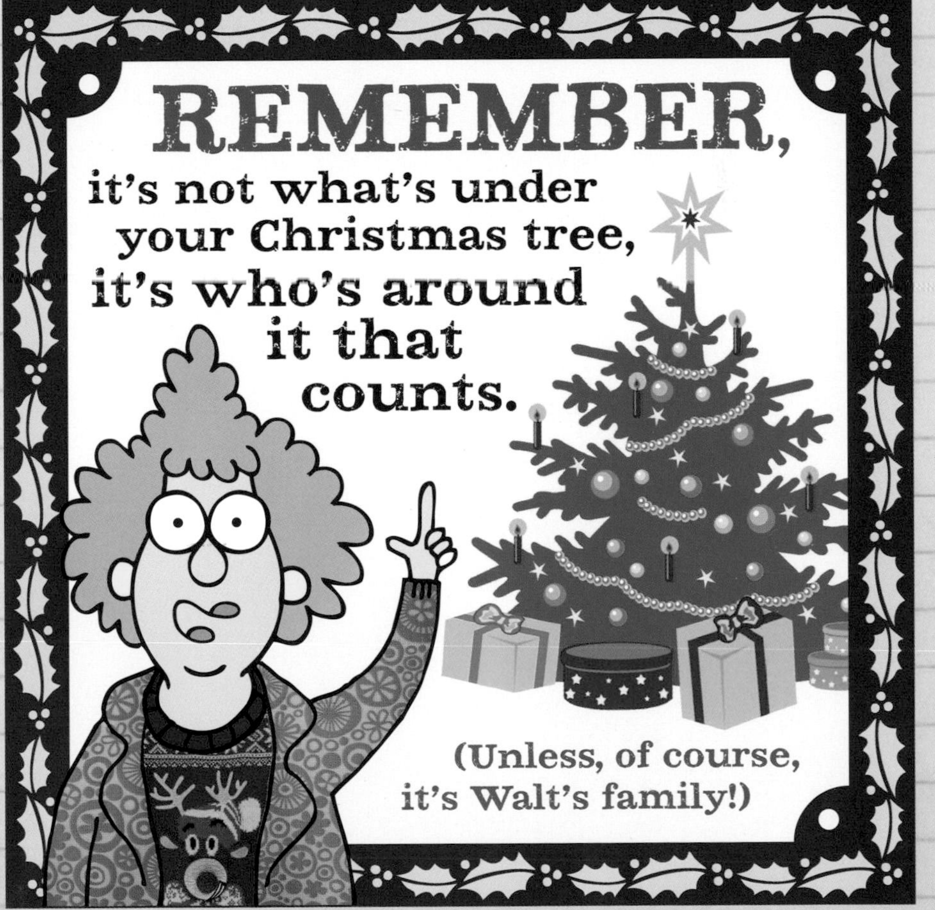
REMEMBER,
it's not what's under your Christmas tree, it's who's around it that counts.
(Unless, of course, it's Walt's family!)

FESTIVE FIRST AID TIP NO.3

My medic-alert bracelet tells it straight: "Scotch only. No smelling salts."

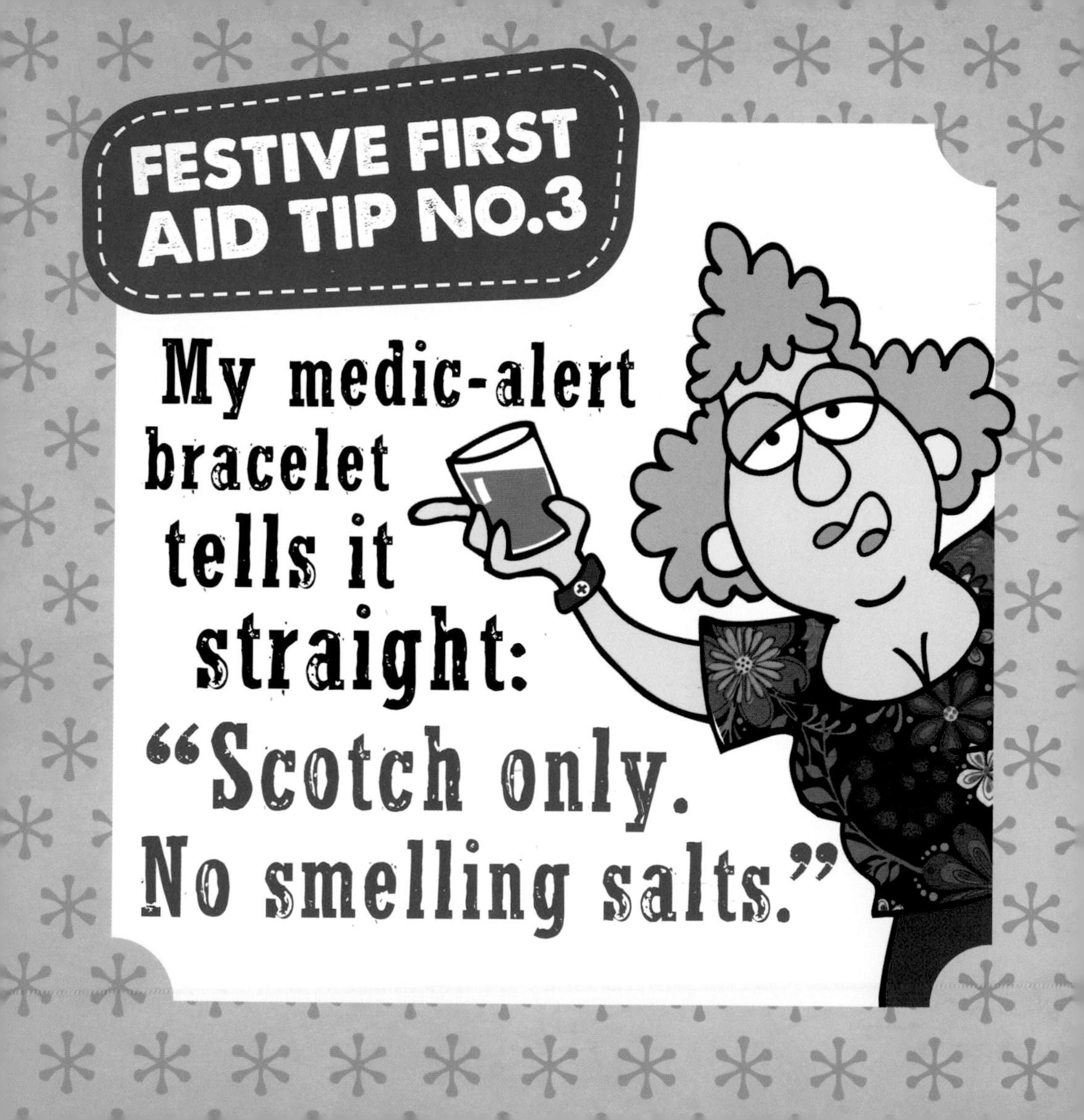

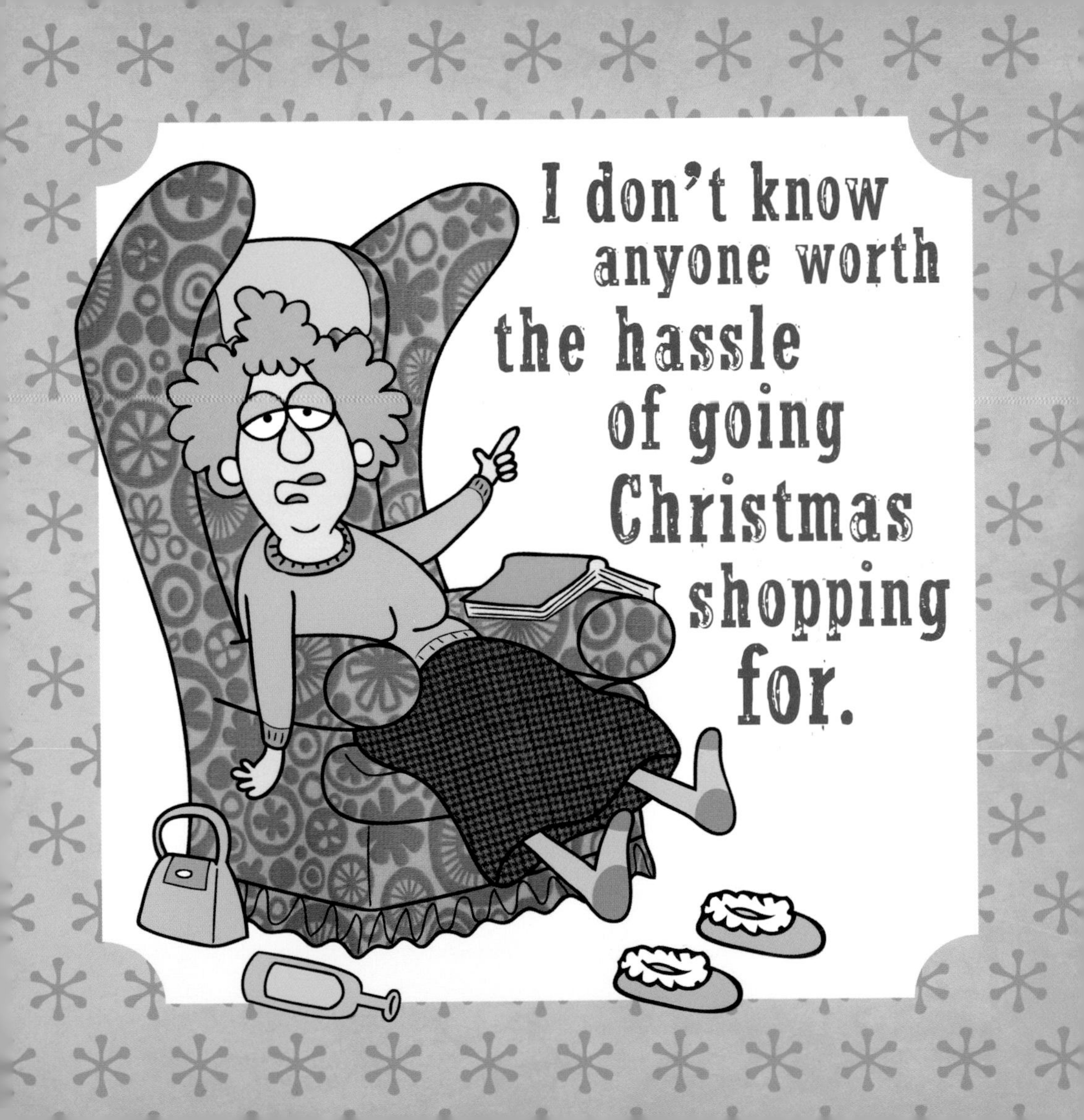

I don't know anyone worth the hassle of going Christmas shopping for.

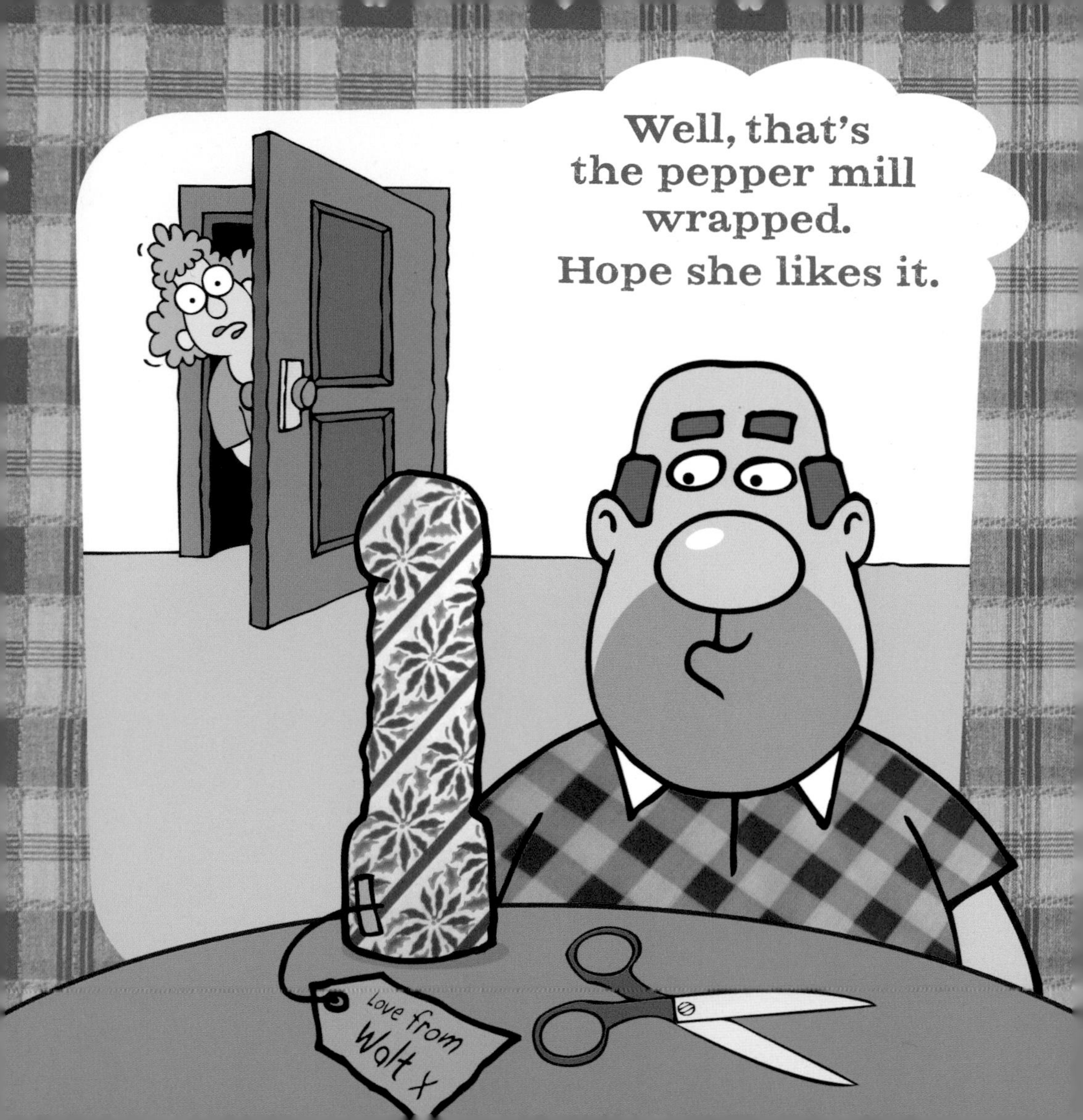
Well, that's the pepper mill wrapped. Hope she likes it.
Love from Walt x

ALL AUNTY WANTS FOR CHRISTMAS

I only want one Christmas gift,
It's the only Christmas wish I've wished.
I just want to know all the names
Of the men on Santa's naughty list!

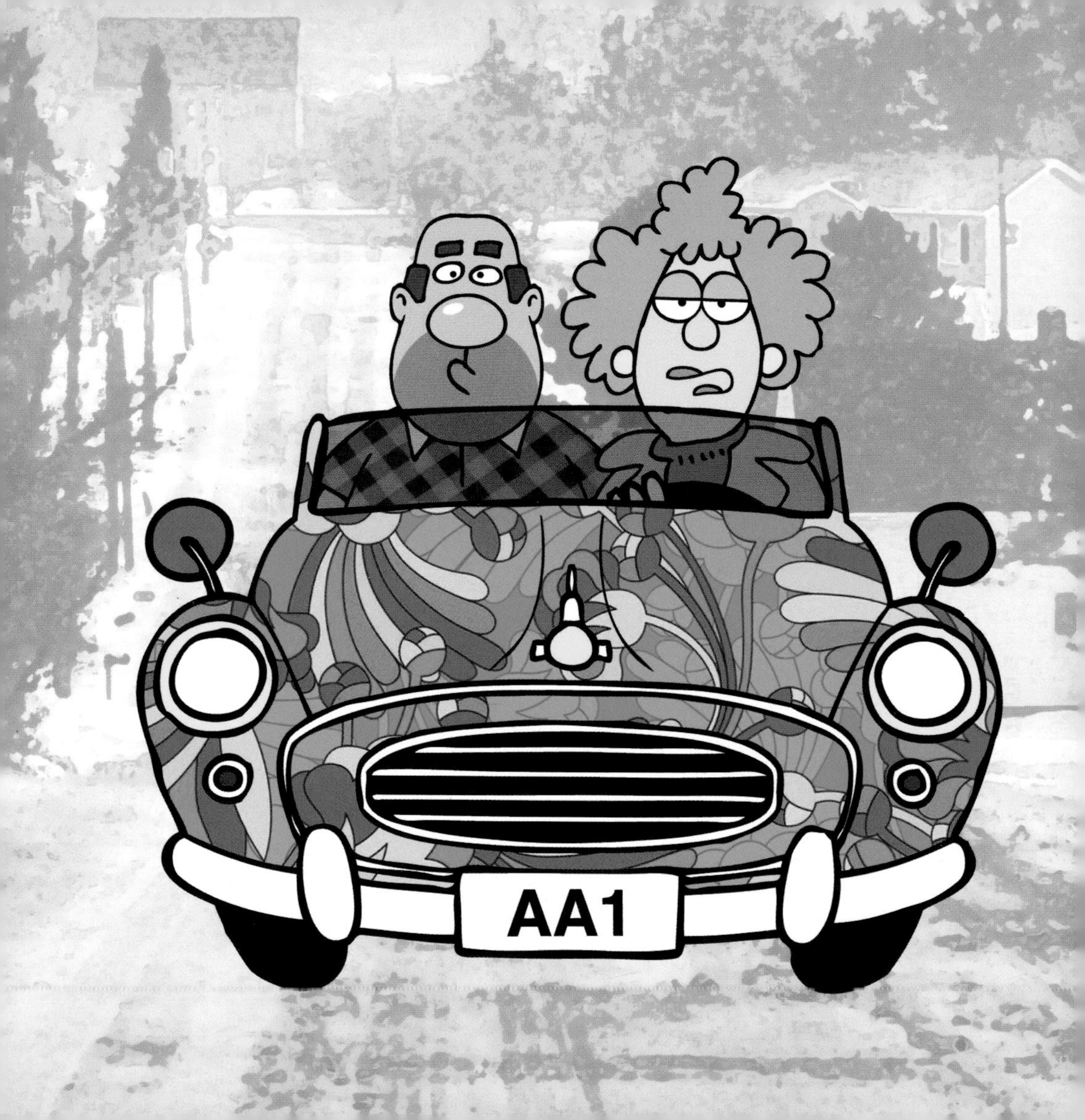
AA1

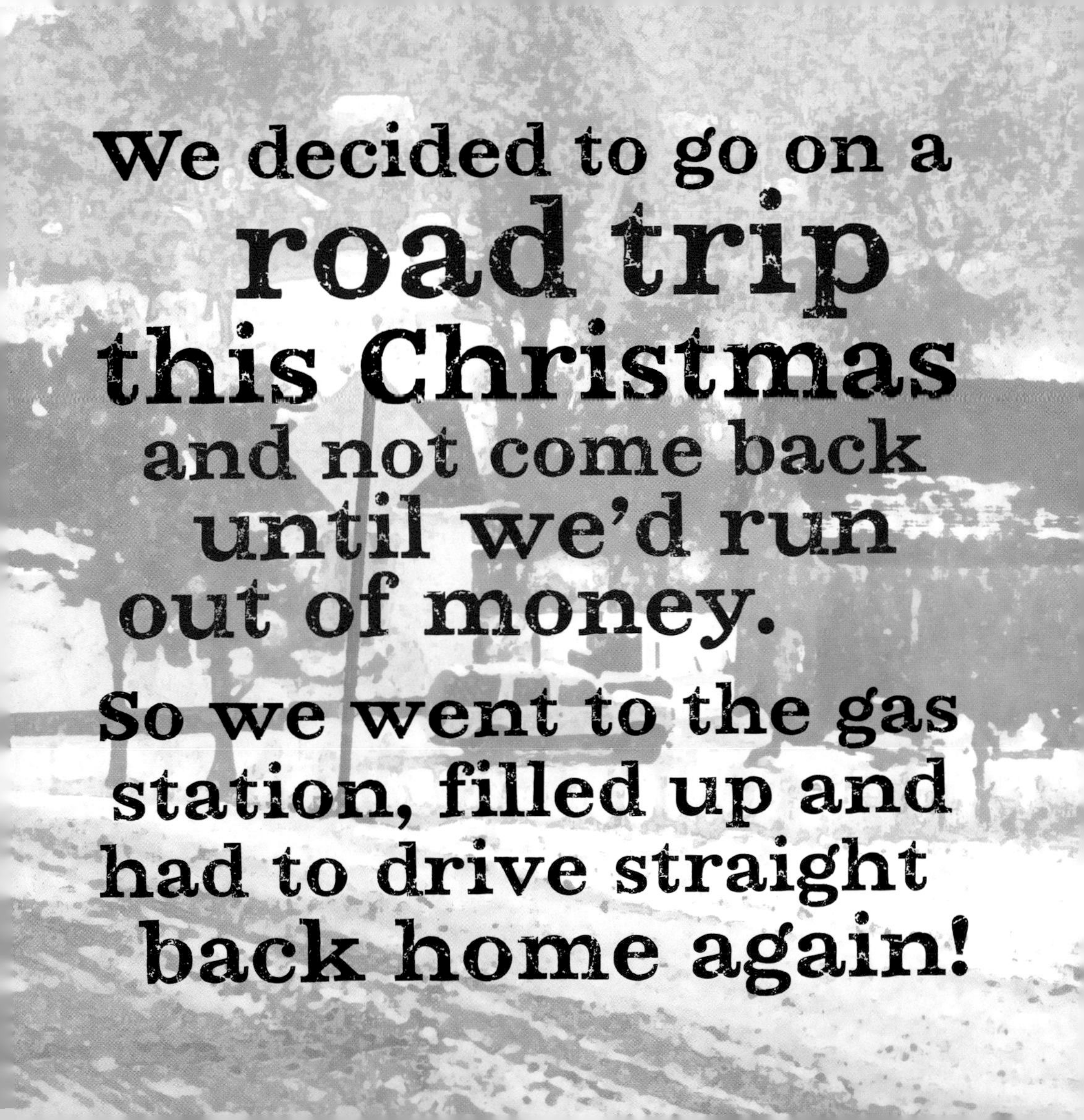

We decided to go on a **road trip** this Christmas and not come back until we'd run out of money.

So we went to the gas station, filled up and had to drive straight back home again!

The trouble with having elves for helpers is they always get IDed when you send them to get booze!

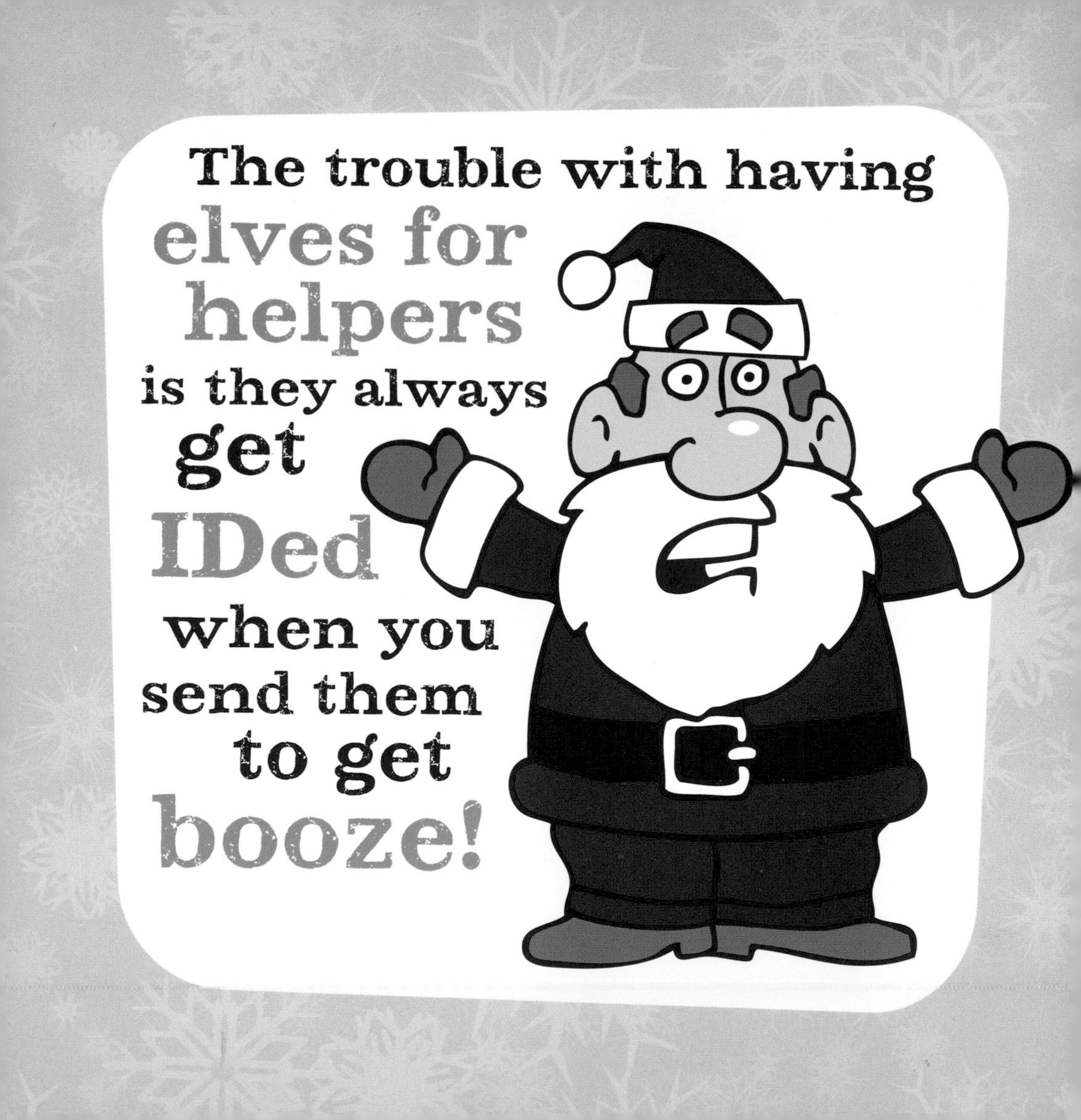

Christmas is a time when you get homesick, even when you are at home.

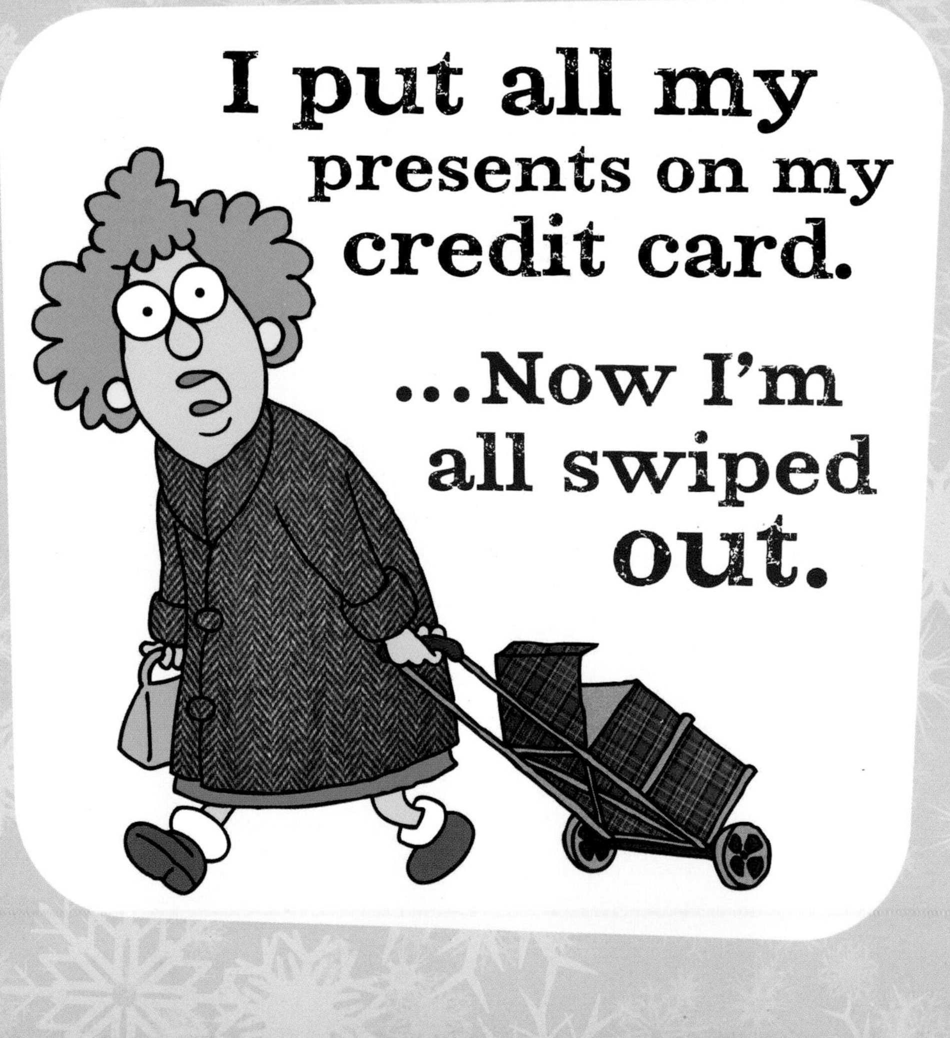
I put all my presents on my credit card.
...Now I'm all swiped out.

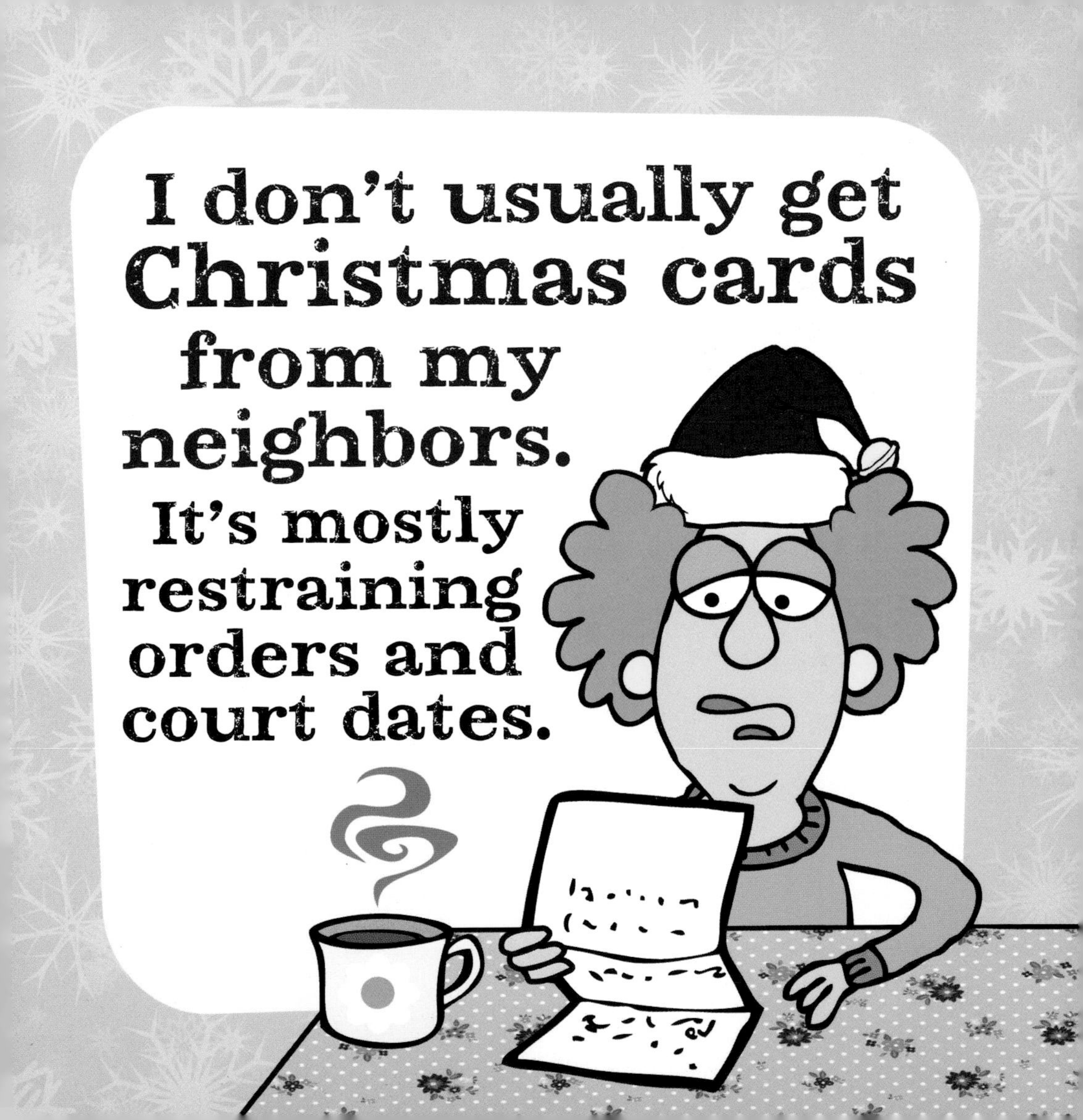
I don't usually get Christmas cards from my neighbors.
It's mostly restraining orders and court dates.

I prepare dinner on Christmas Eve...

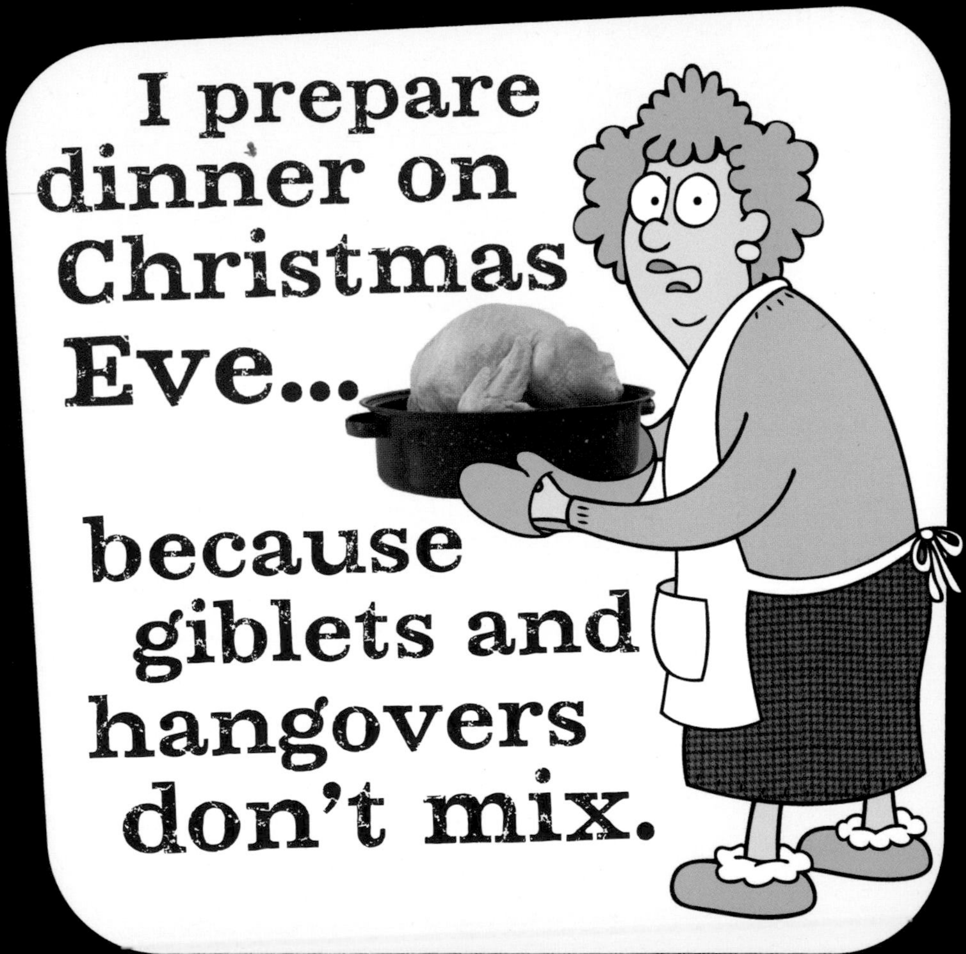

because giblets and hangovers don't mix.

My Christmas tree looks better than **ME** with the lights on.

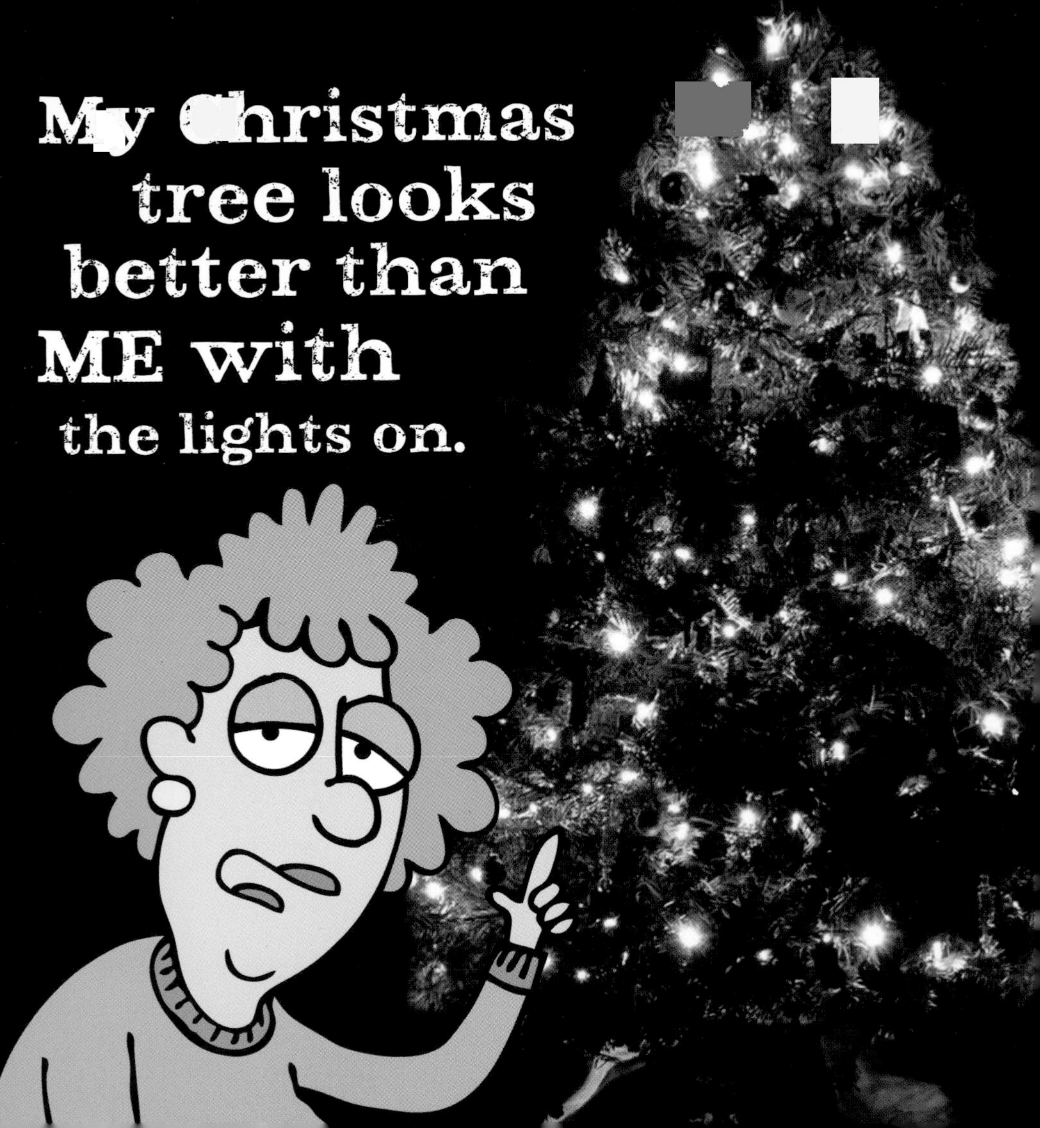

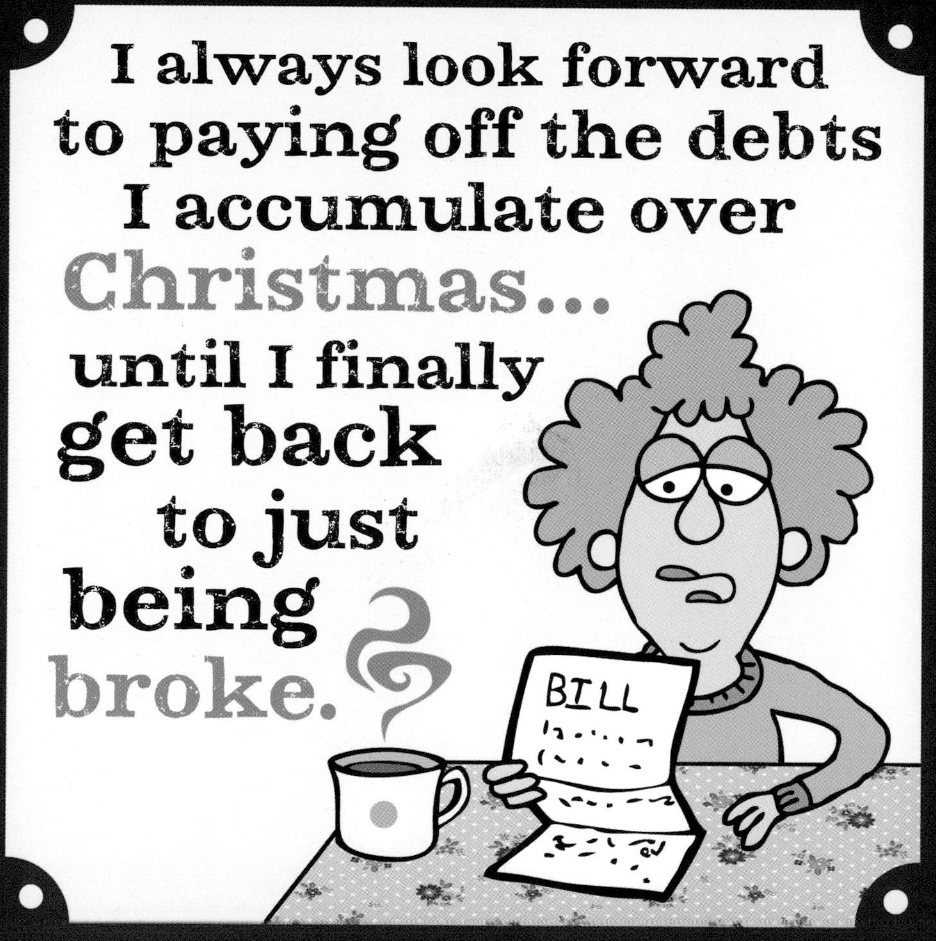
I always look forward to paying off the debts I accumulate over Christmas... until I finally get back to just being broke.
BILL

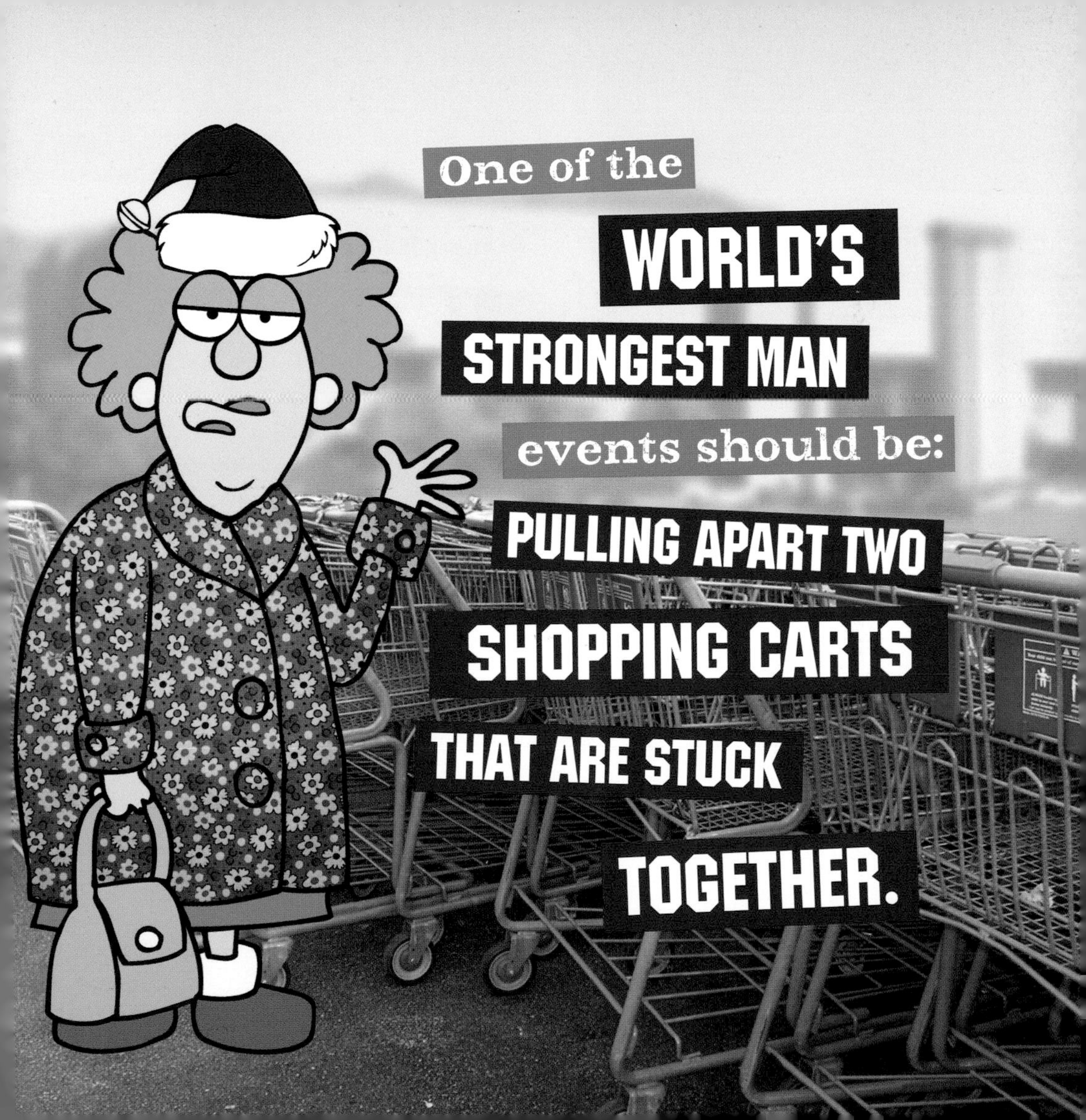
One of the
WORLD'S
STRONGEST MAN
events should be:
PULLING APART TWO
SHOPPING CARTS
THAT ARE STUCK
TOGETHER.

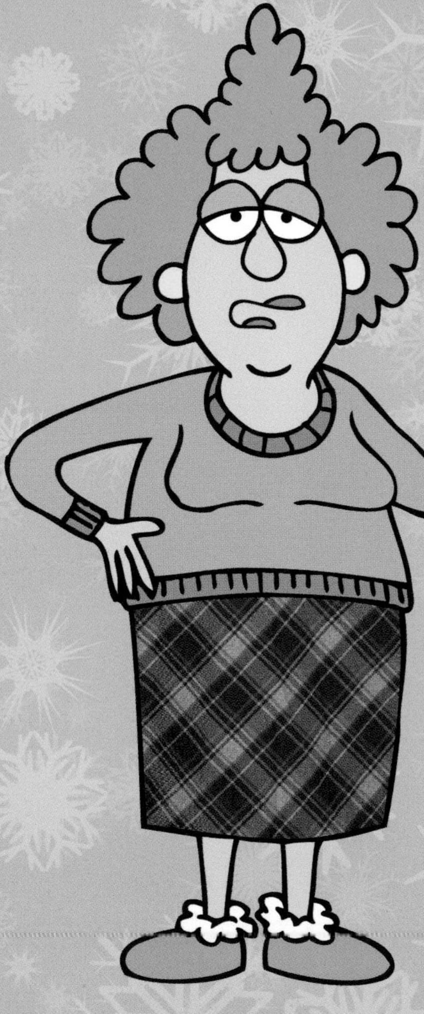

I want to live in a state that lets you shoot carol singers.

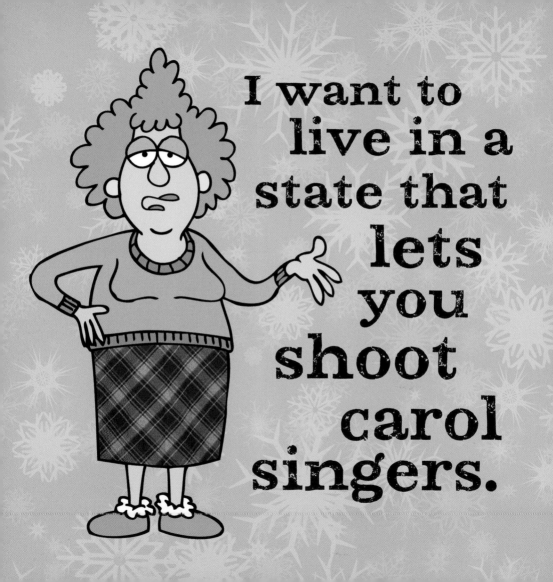

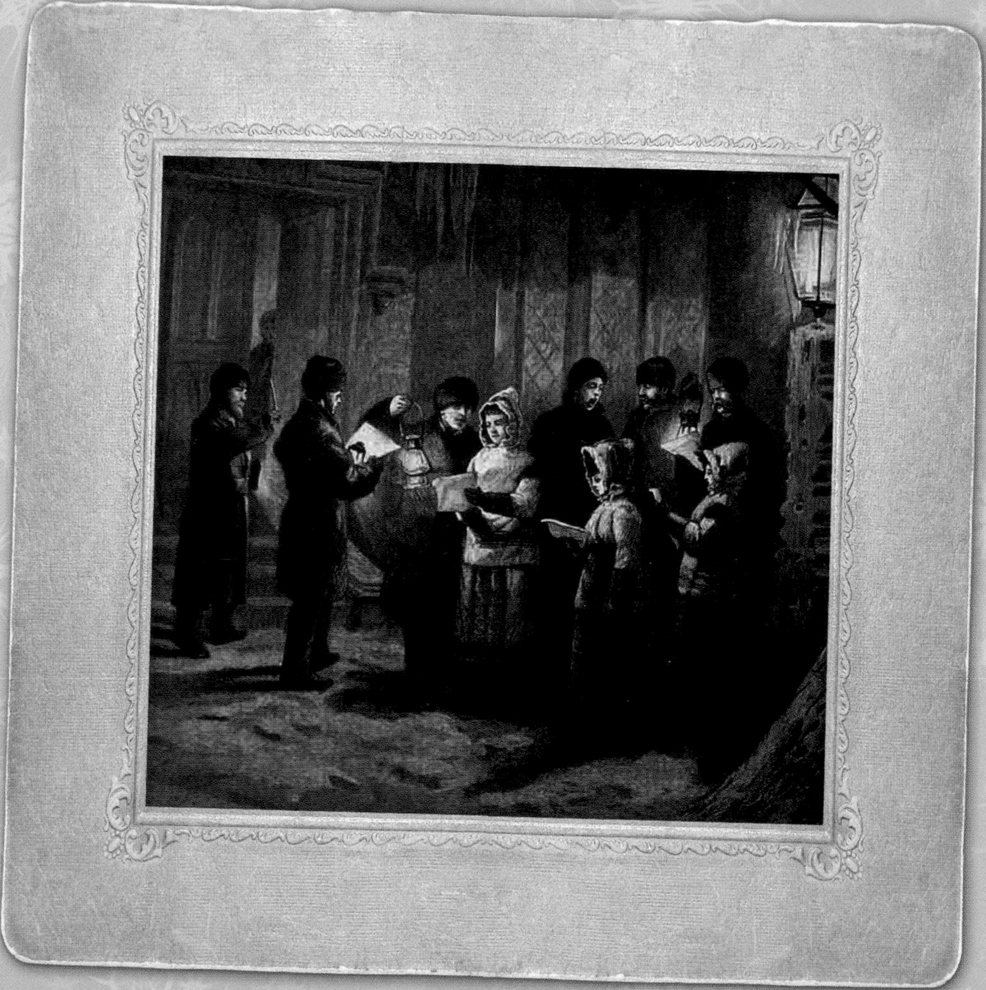

Festive Aerobics

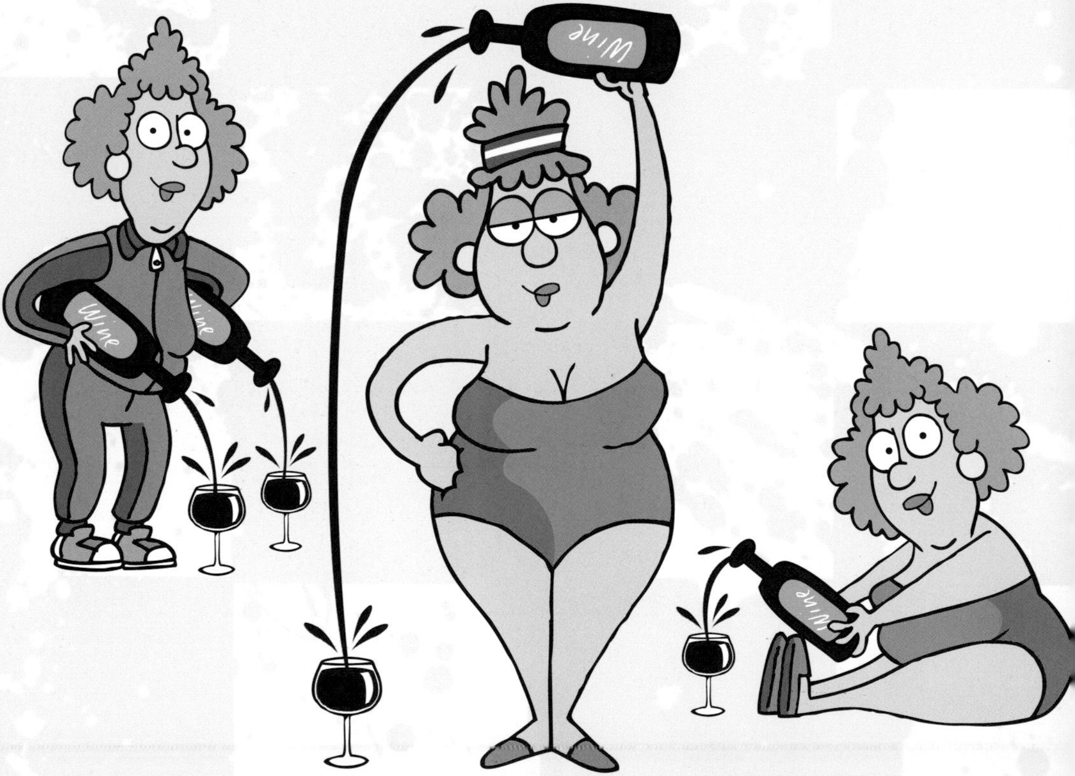

Wine
Wine
Wine
Wine

for the Wine Lover

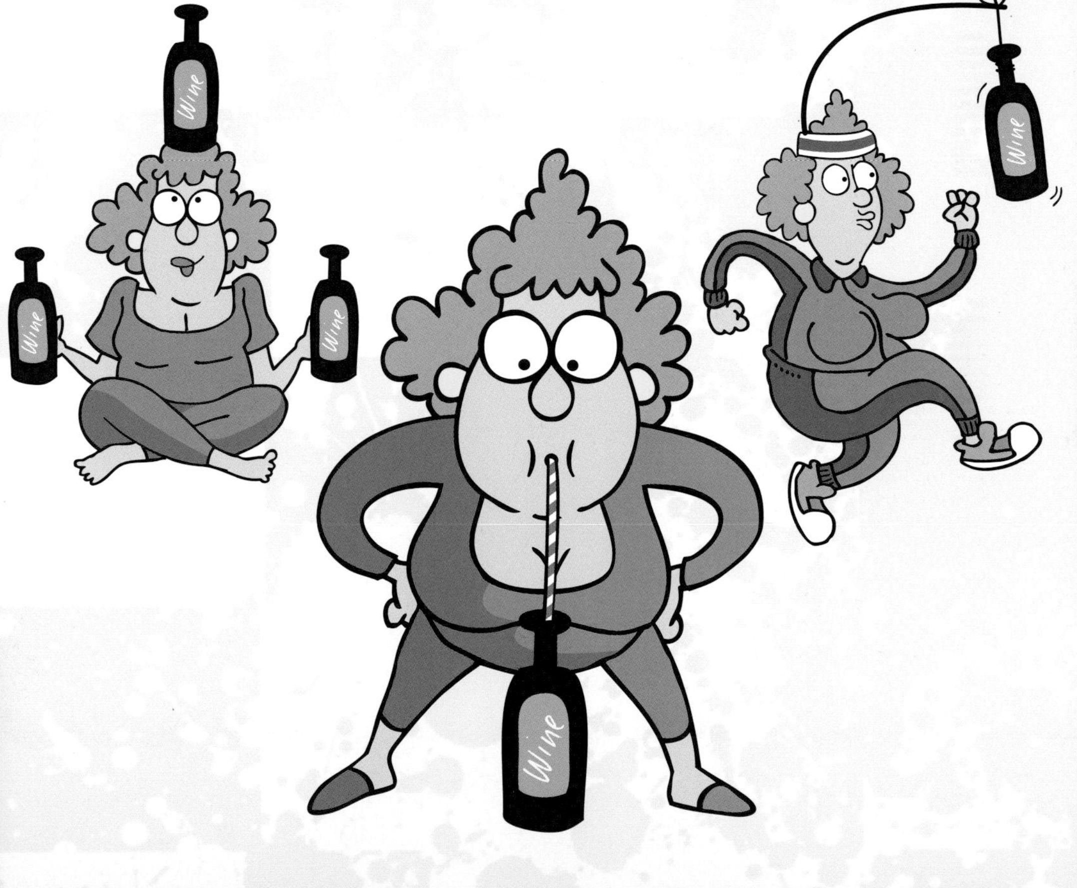
Wine
Wine
Wine
Wine
Wine

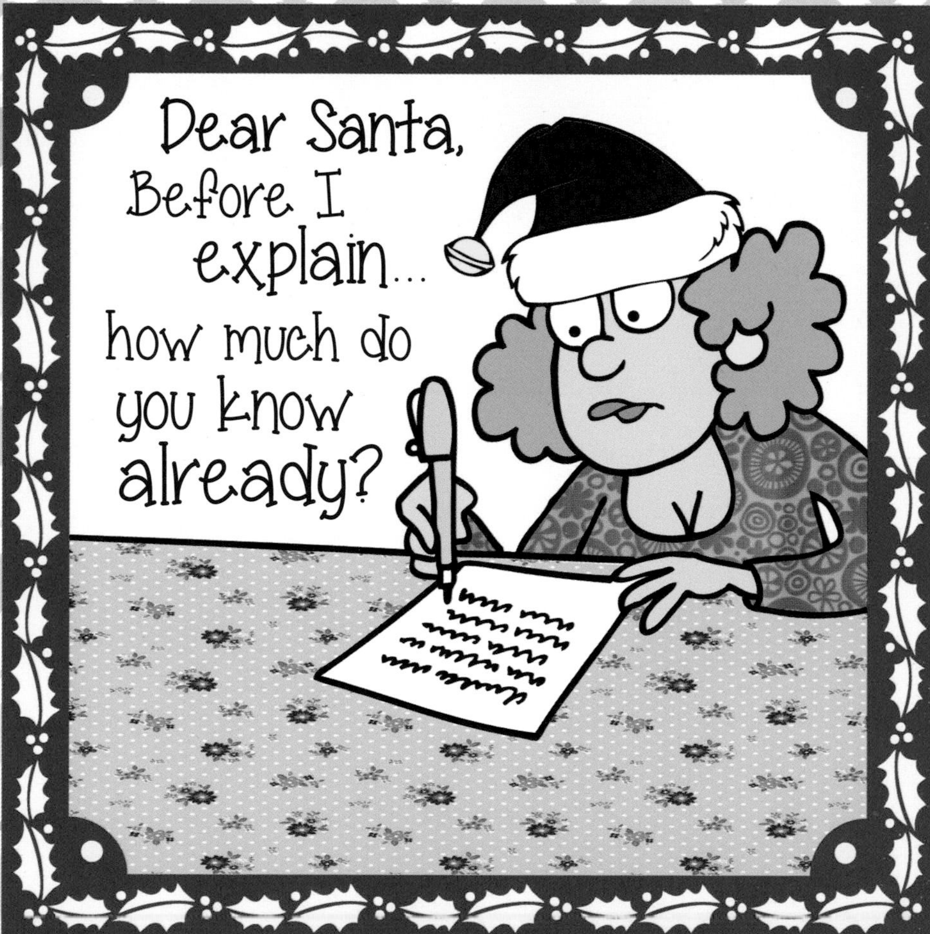
Dear Santa,
Before I explain...
how much do you know already?

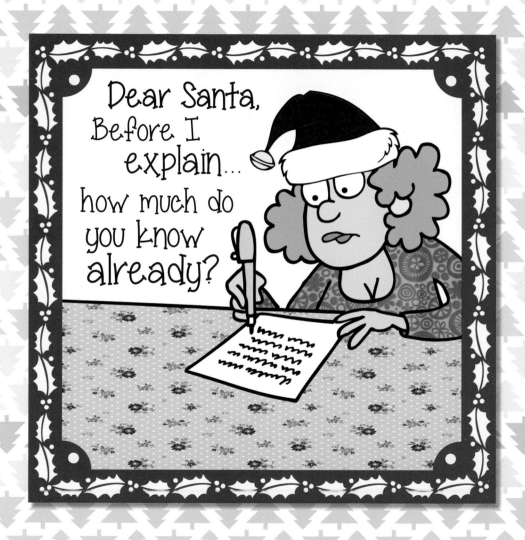

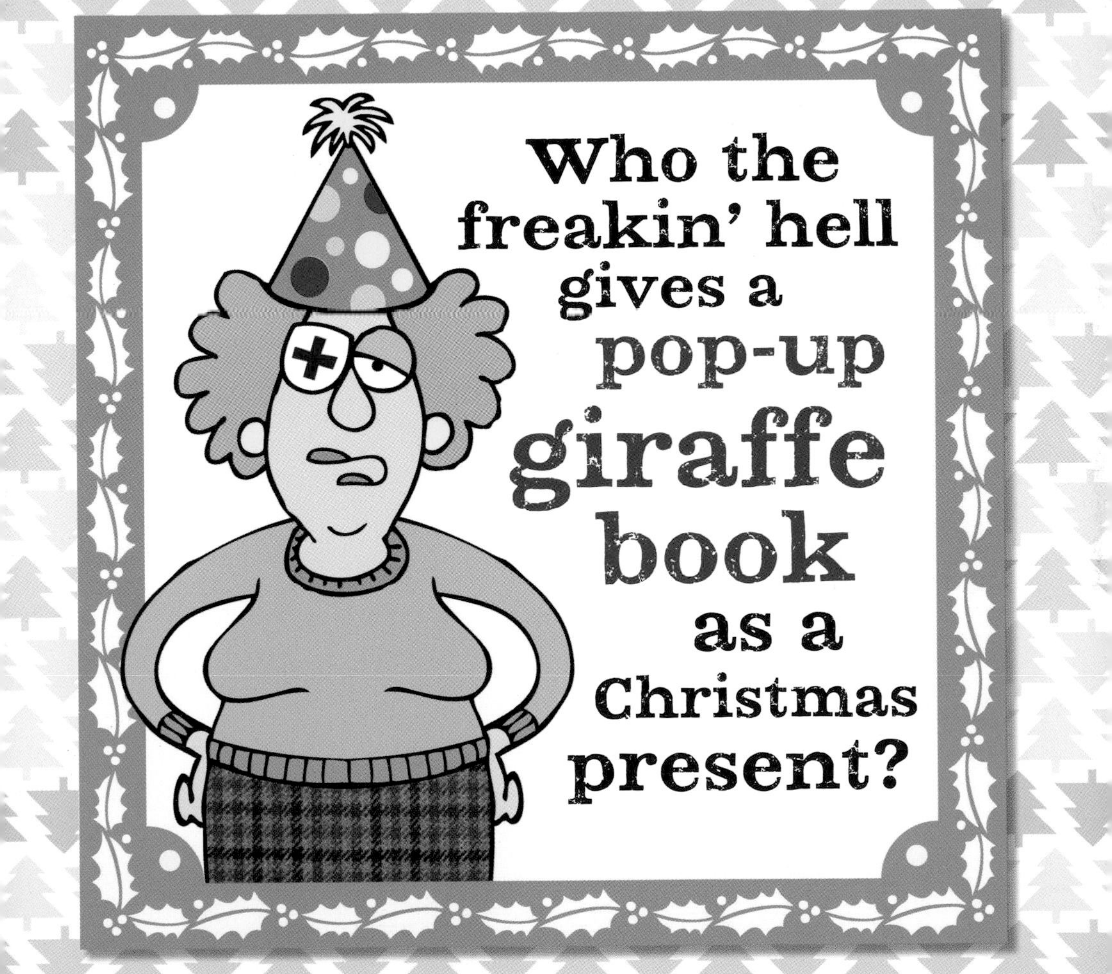

Who the freakin' hell gives a pop-up giraffe book as a Christmas present?

We invested in a set of "energy saving" tree lights this year.

By the time they lit up, it was time to take the freakin' tree down!

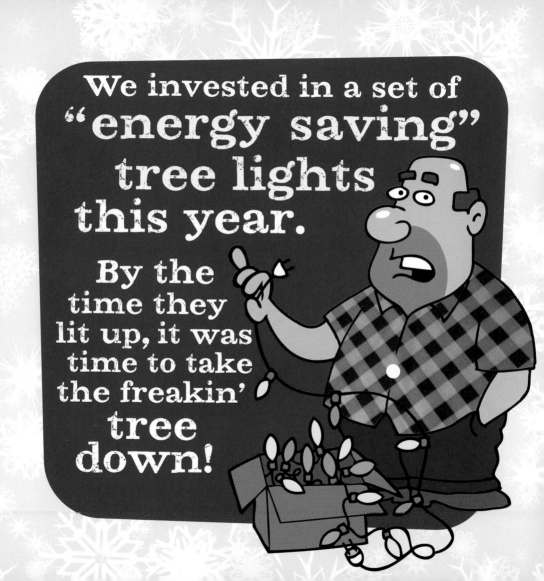

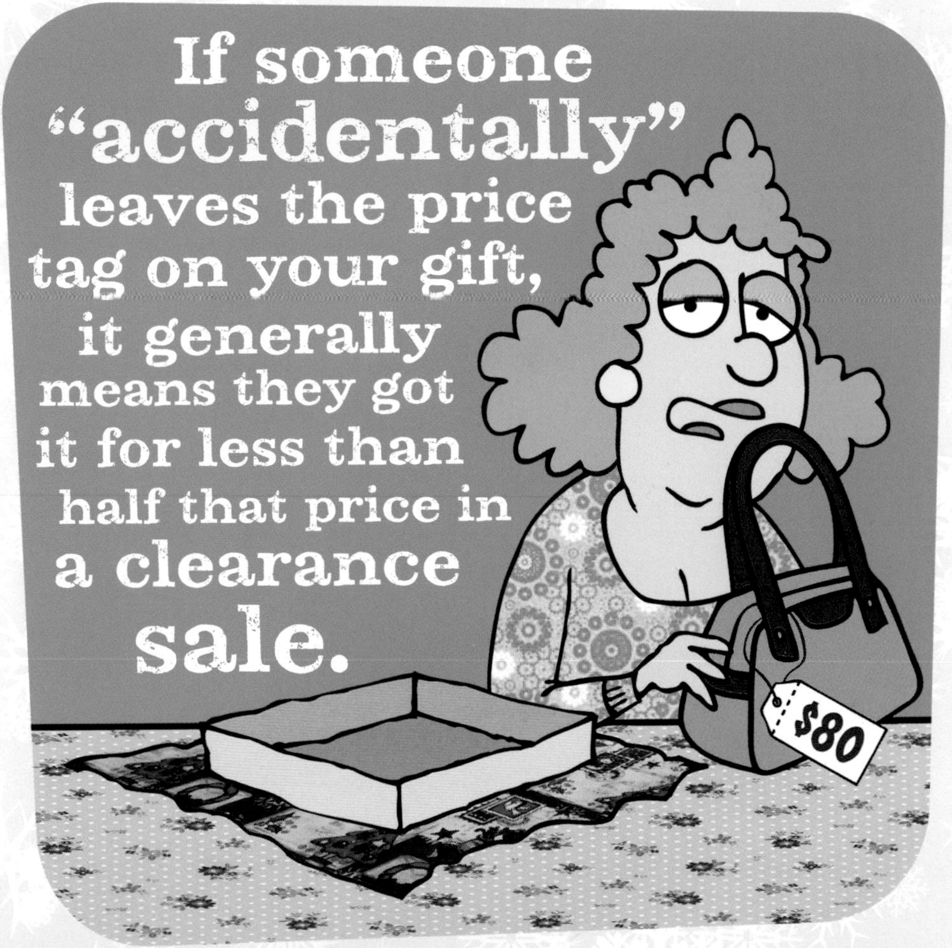
If someone "accidentally" leaves the price tag on your gift, it generally means they got it for less than half that price in a clearance sale.
$80

My mother-in-law is worried about me cooking Christmas dinner this year.

I told her not to worry—many people have eaten in this kitchen and gone on to live normal, healthy lives.

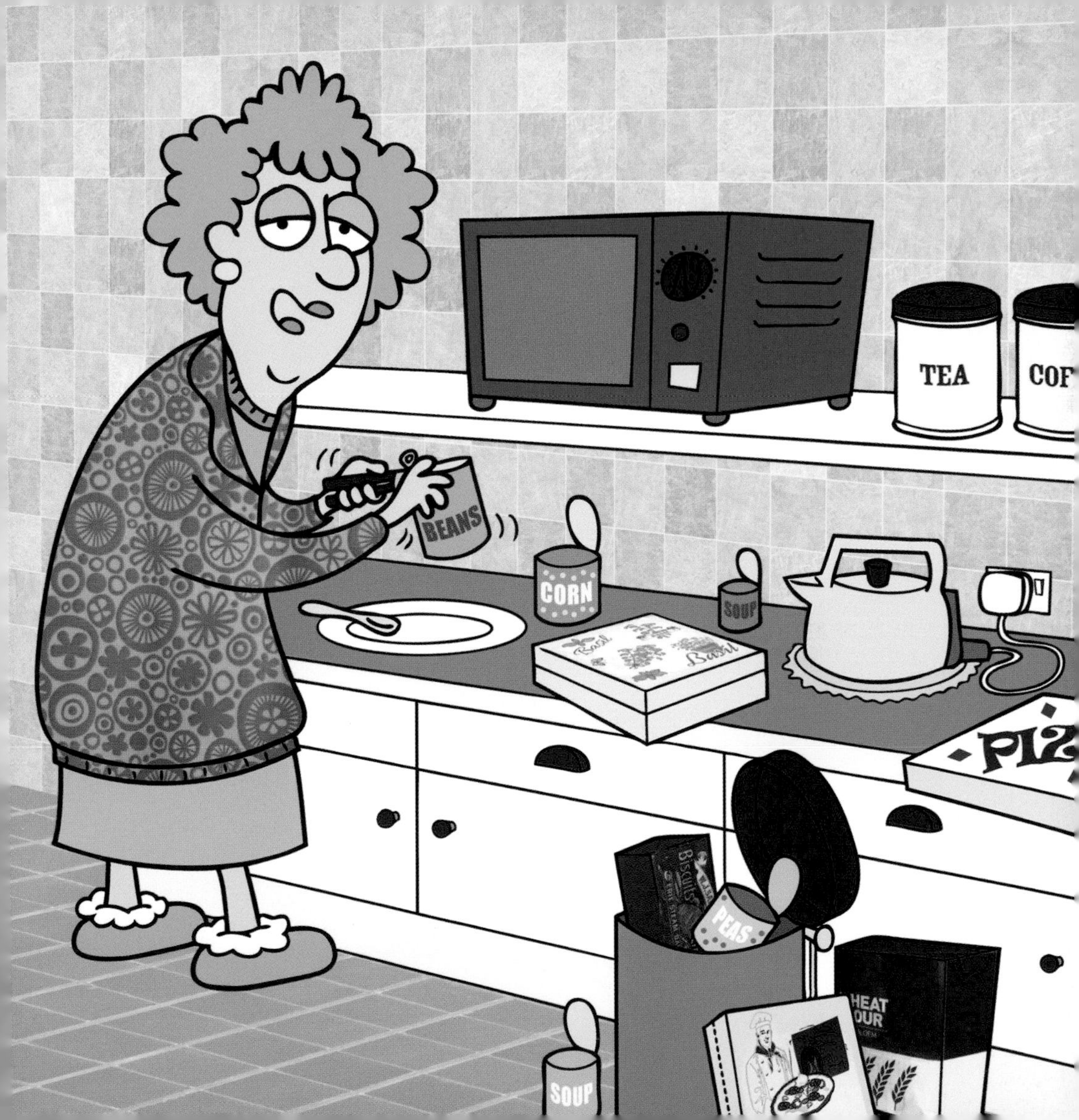
TEA
COF
BEANS
CORN
SOUP
Basil
Basil
PIZ
Biscuits
PEAS
HEAT
OUR
SOUP

It's not the 1950s.

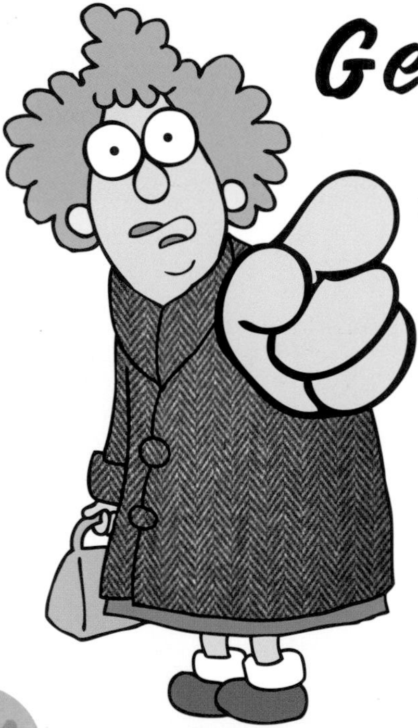

Get off your

ASS

AND COOK YOUR

OWN

Christmas dinner!

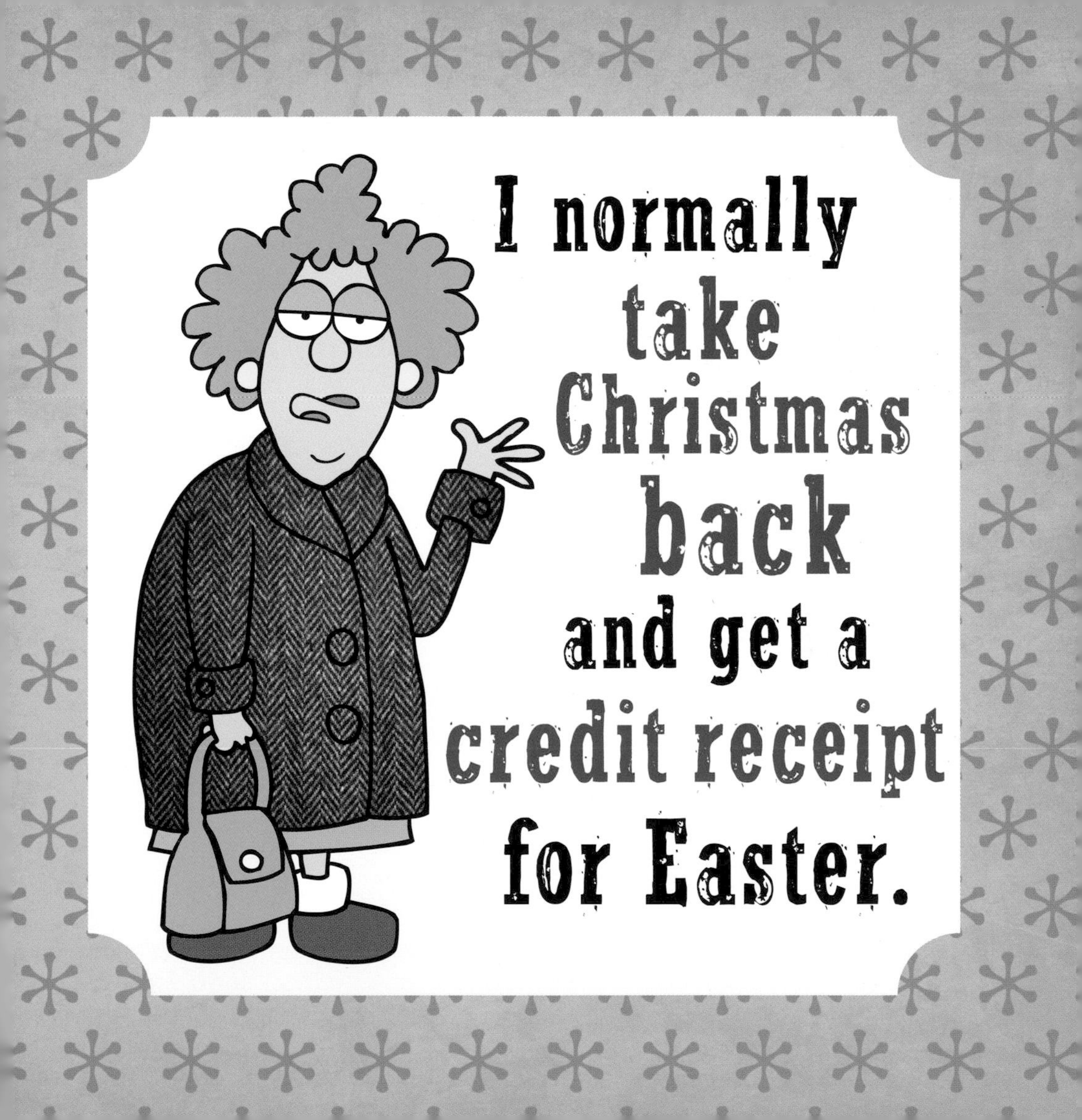

I normally take Christmas back and get a credit receipt for Easter.

CHRISTMAS TIP NO. 3

Don't clear snow off your path; walk in backwards.

That way any visitors will think you're out.

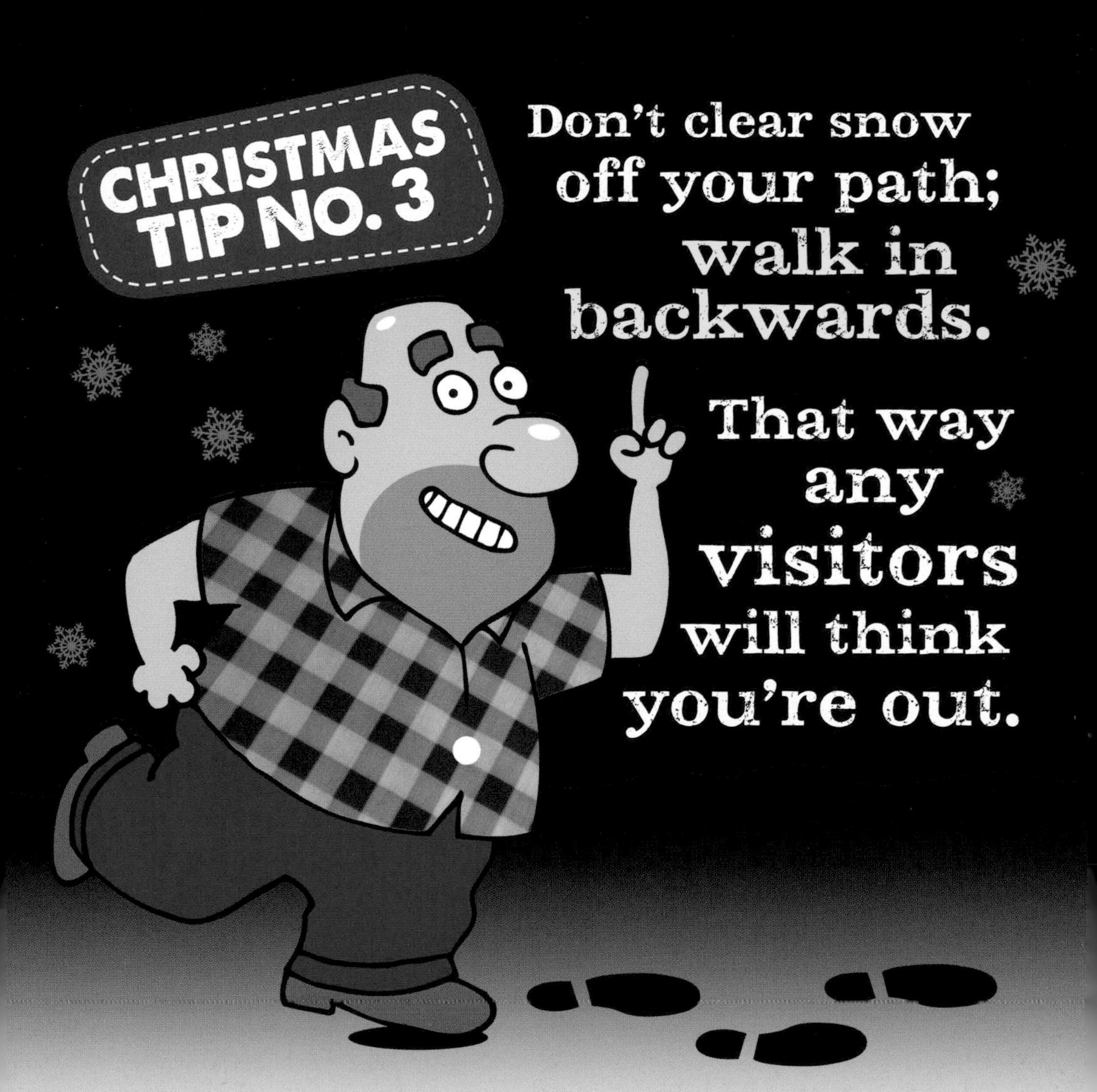

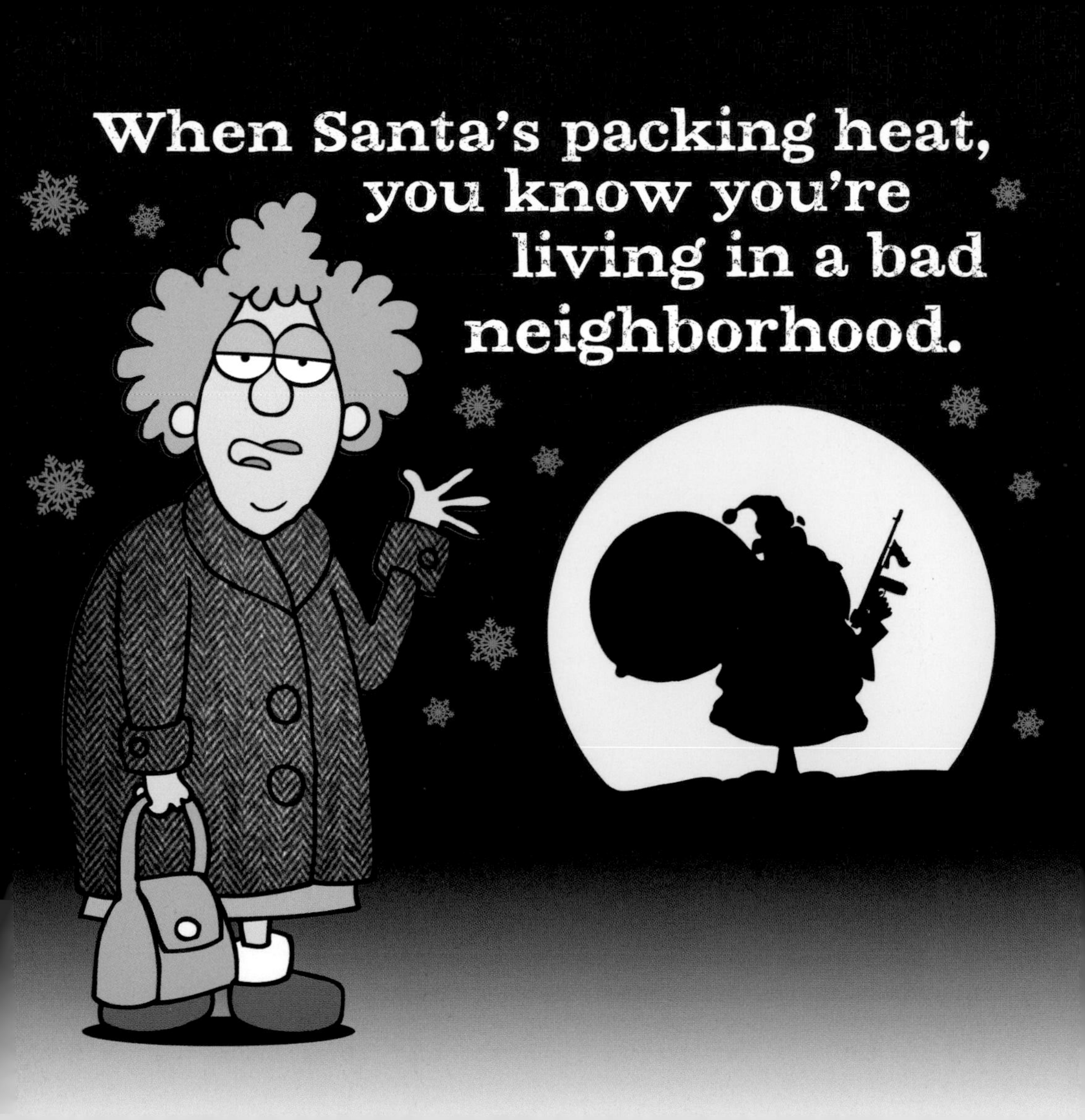
When Santa's packing heat, you know you're living in a bad neighborhood.

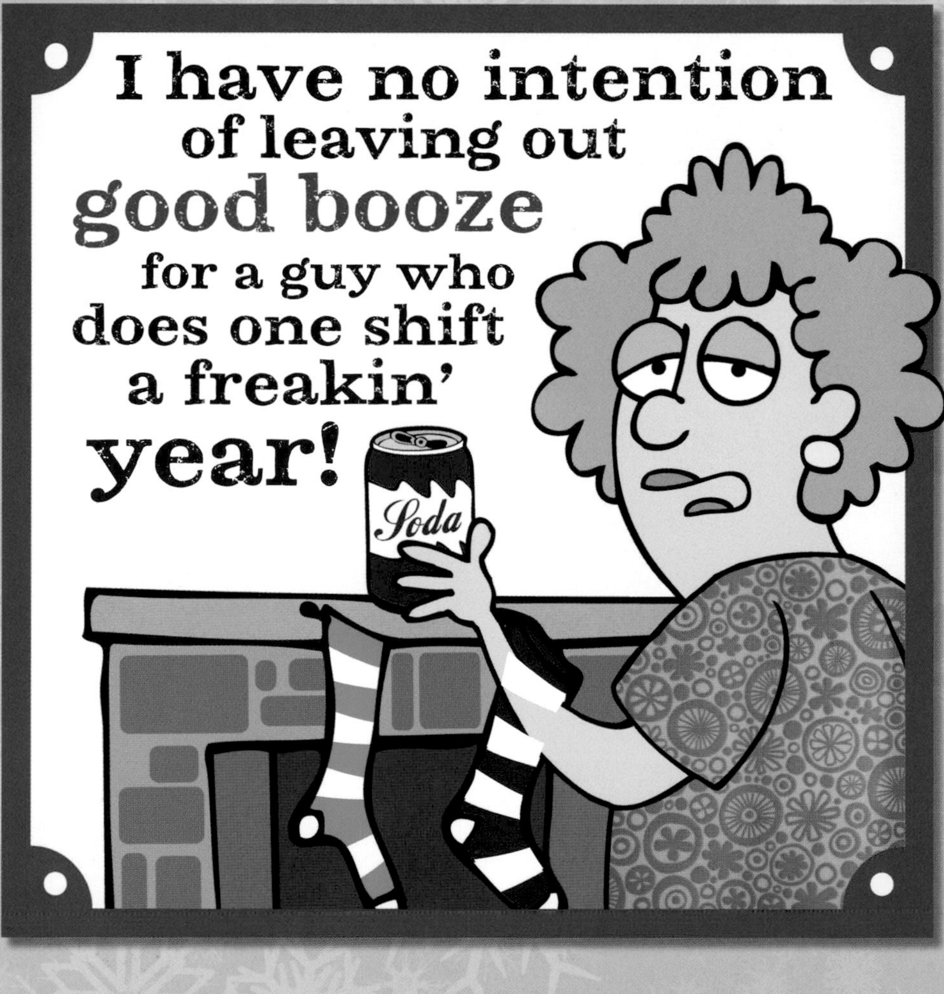
I have no intention of leaving out good booze for a guy who does one shift a freakin' year!
Soda

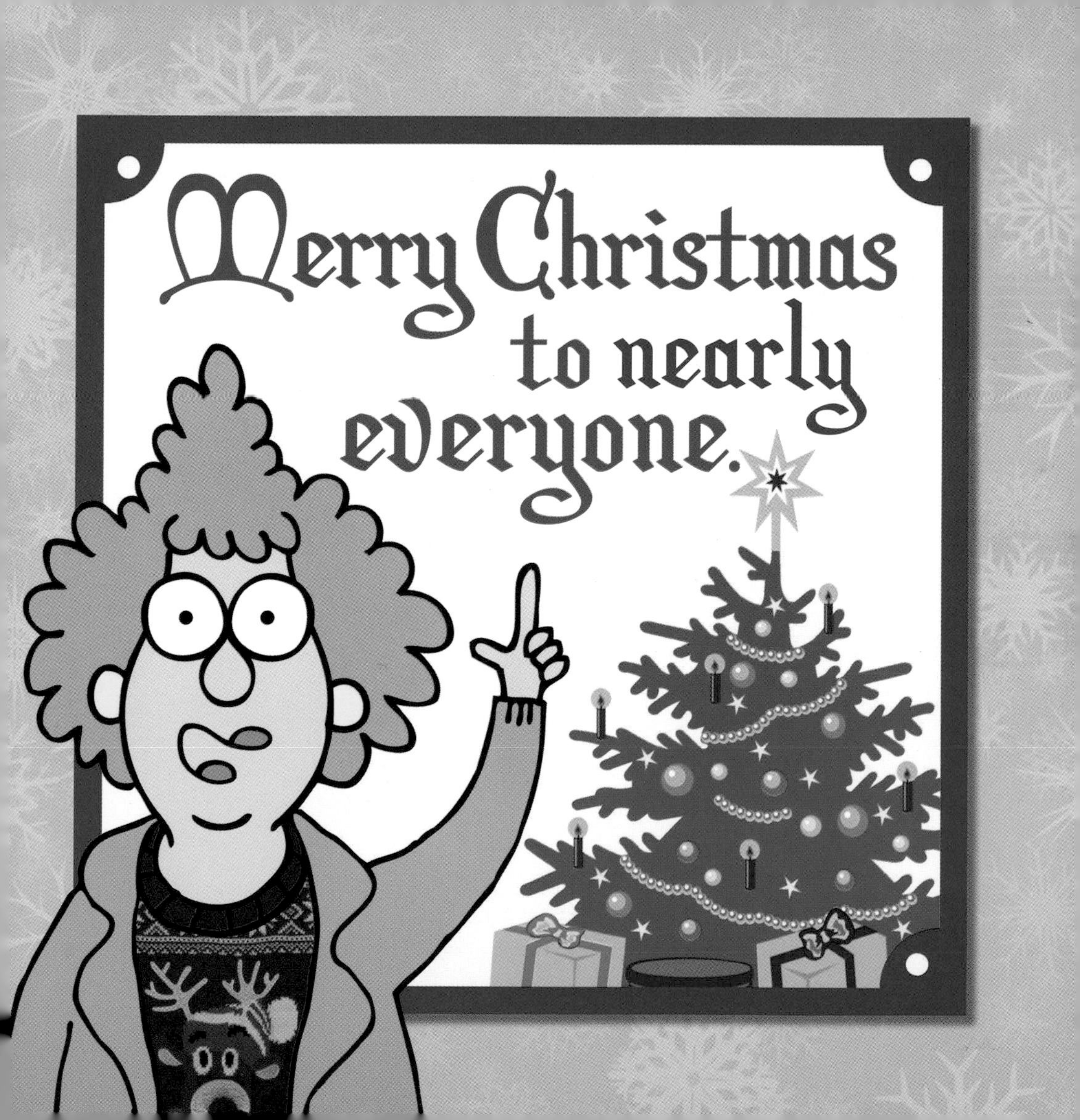
Merry Christmas to nearly everyone.

Christmas is a race to see which gives out first... your money or your freakin' feet.

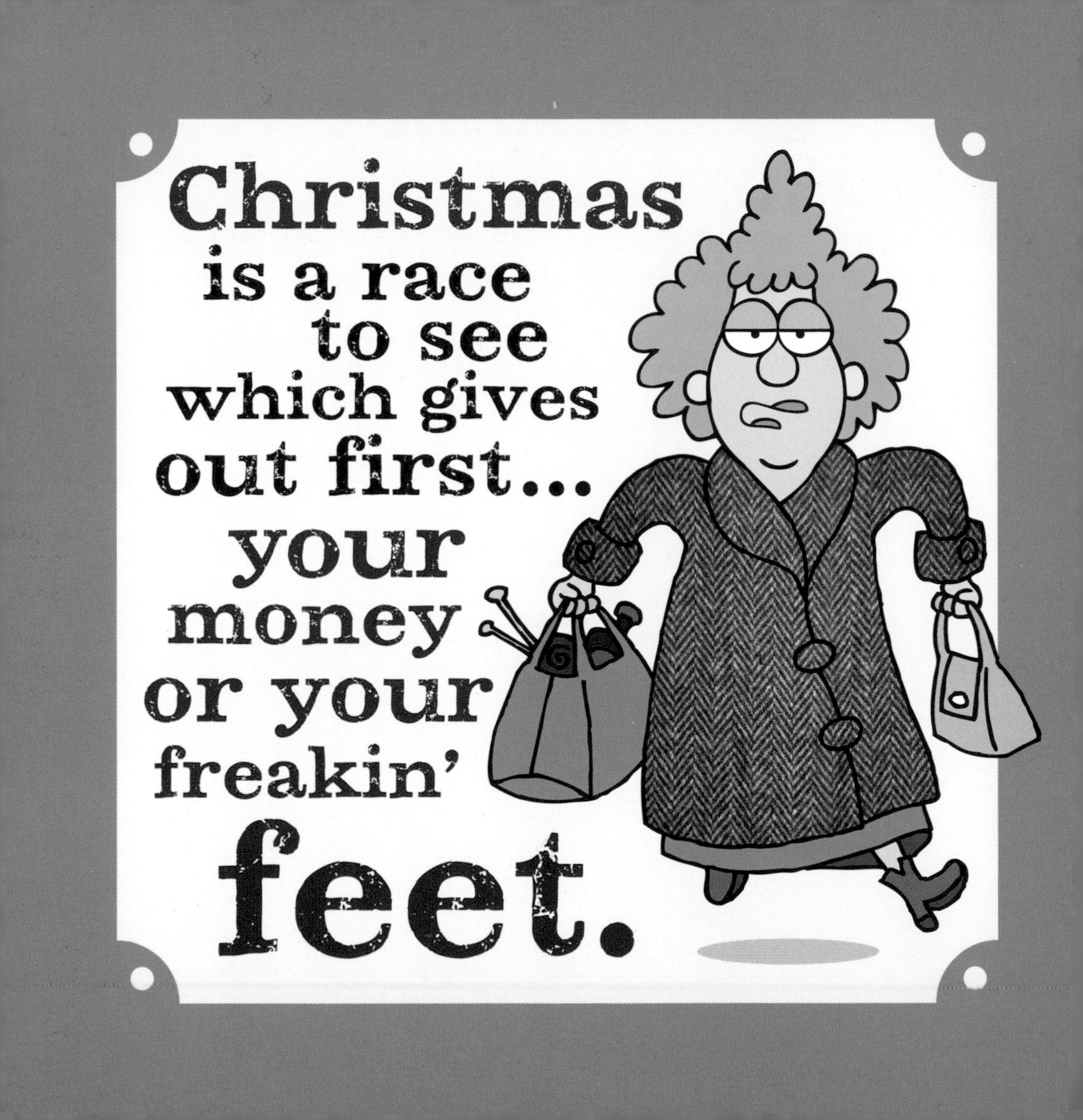

Here's to a
white
Christmas

...and when
we run out
of white,
we'll start
on the red.

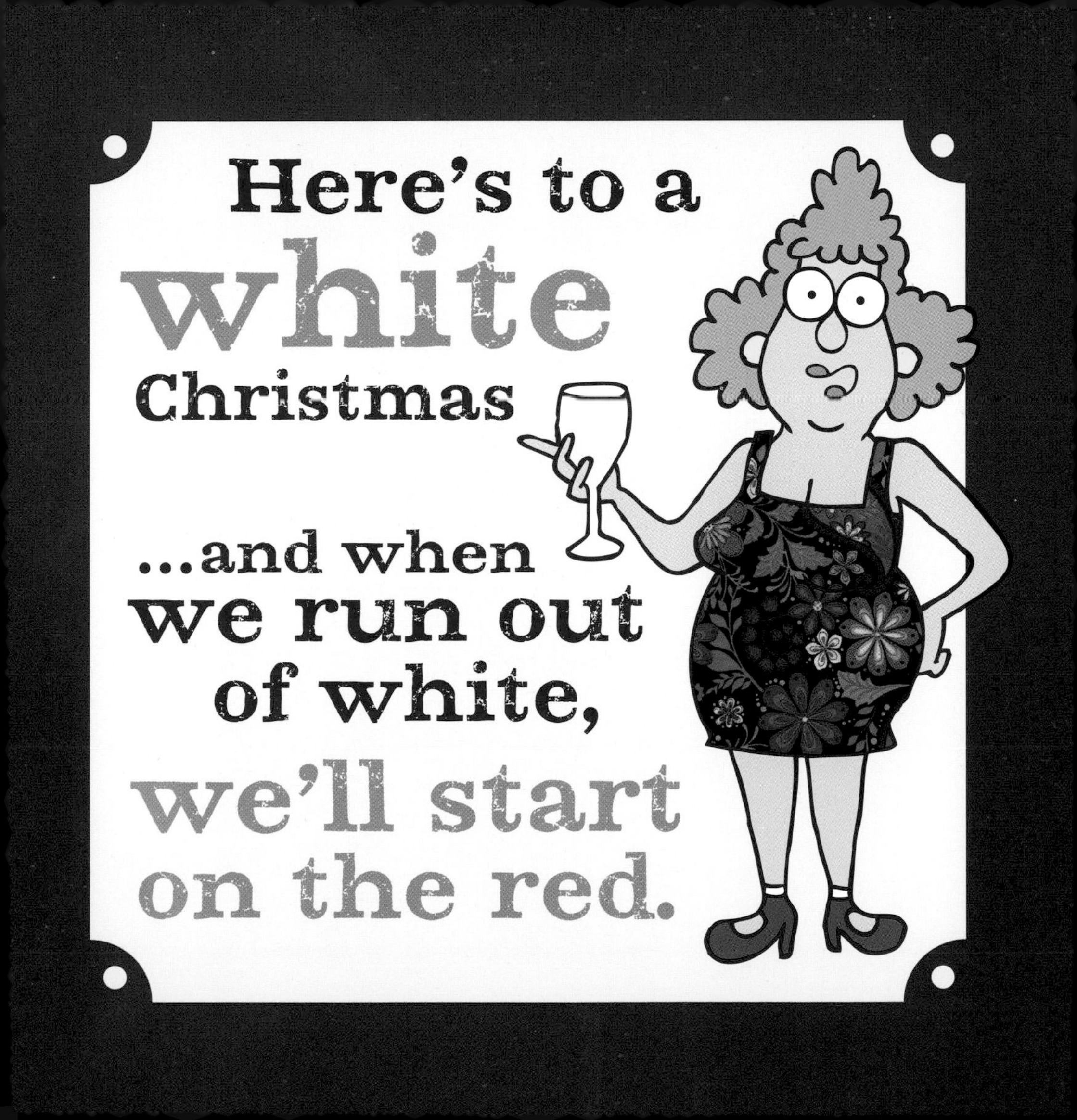

It's Christmas again...

here we go buying this year's gifts with next year's money.

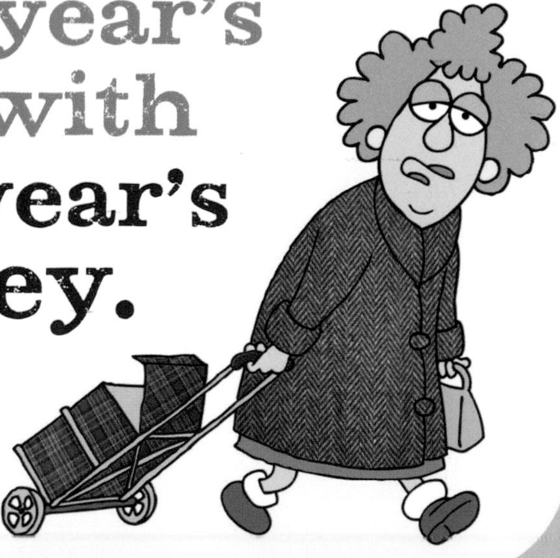

This year I'm going to hang **mistletoe** from my back pocket... so that all the people who annoy me can **kiss my ass.**

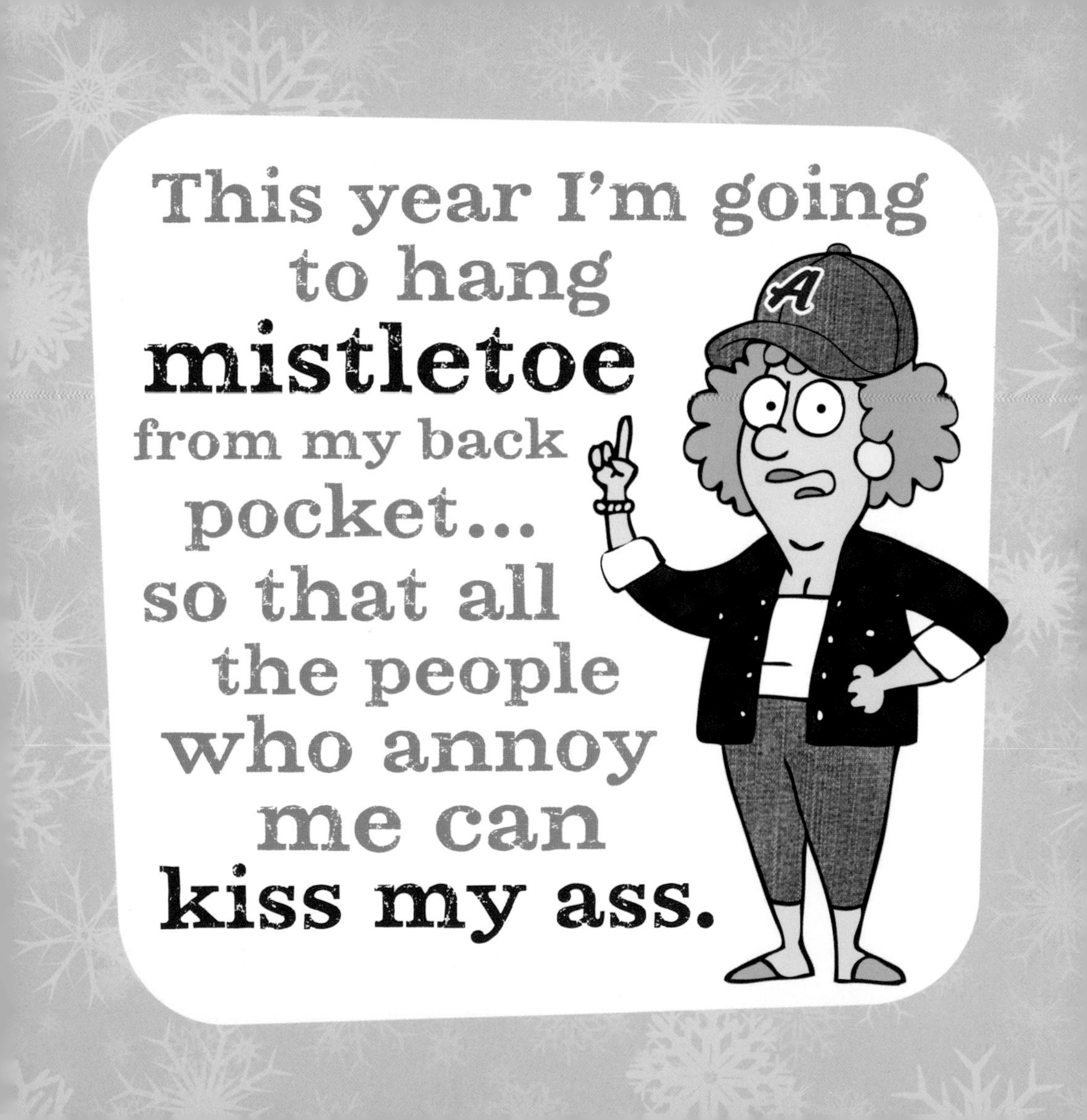

A

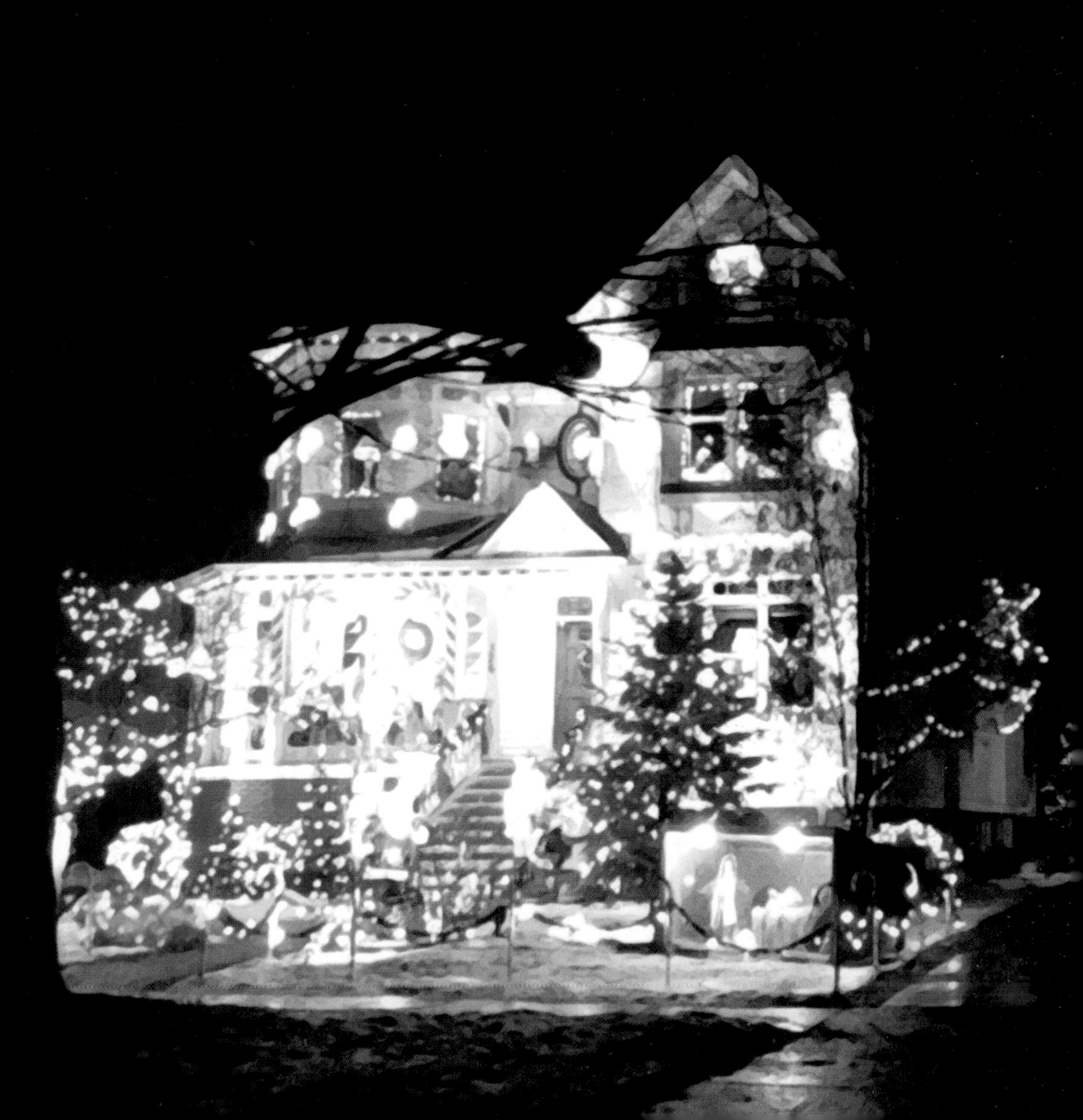

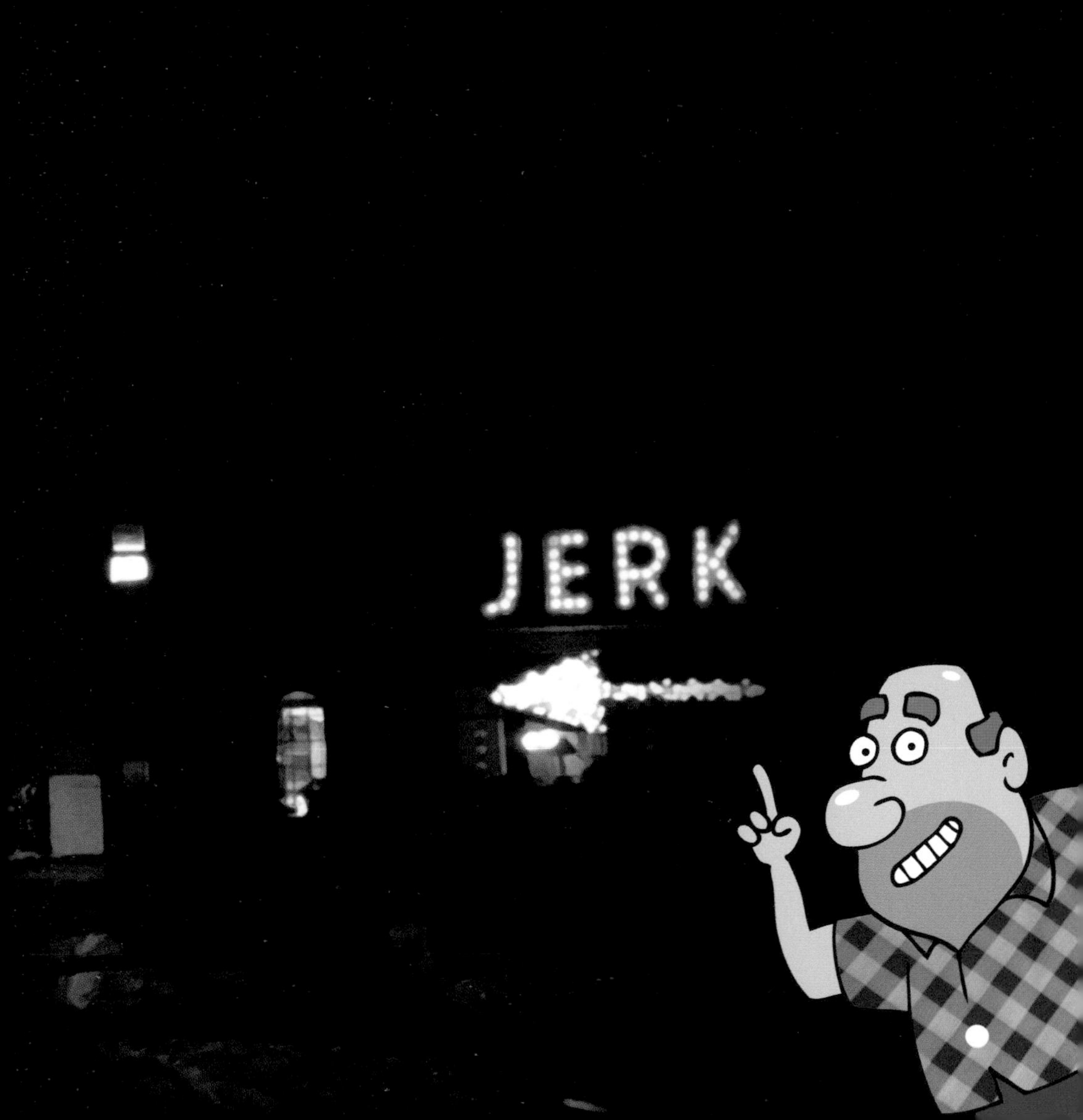
JERK

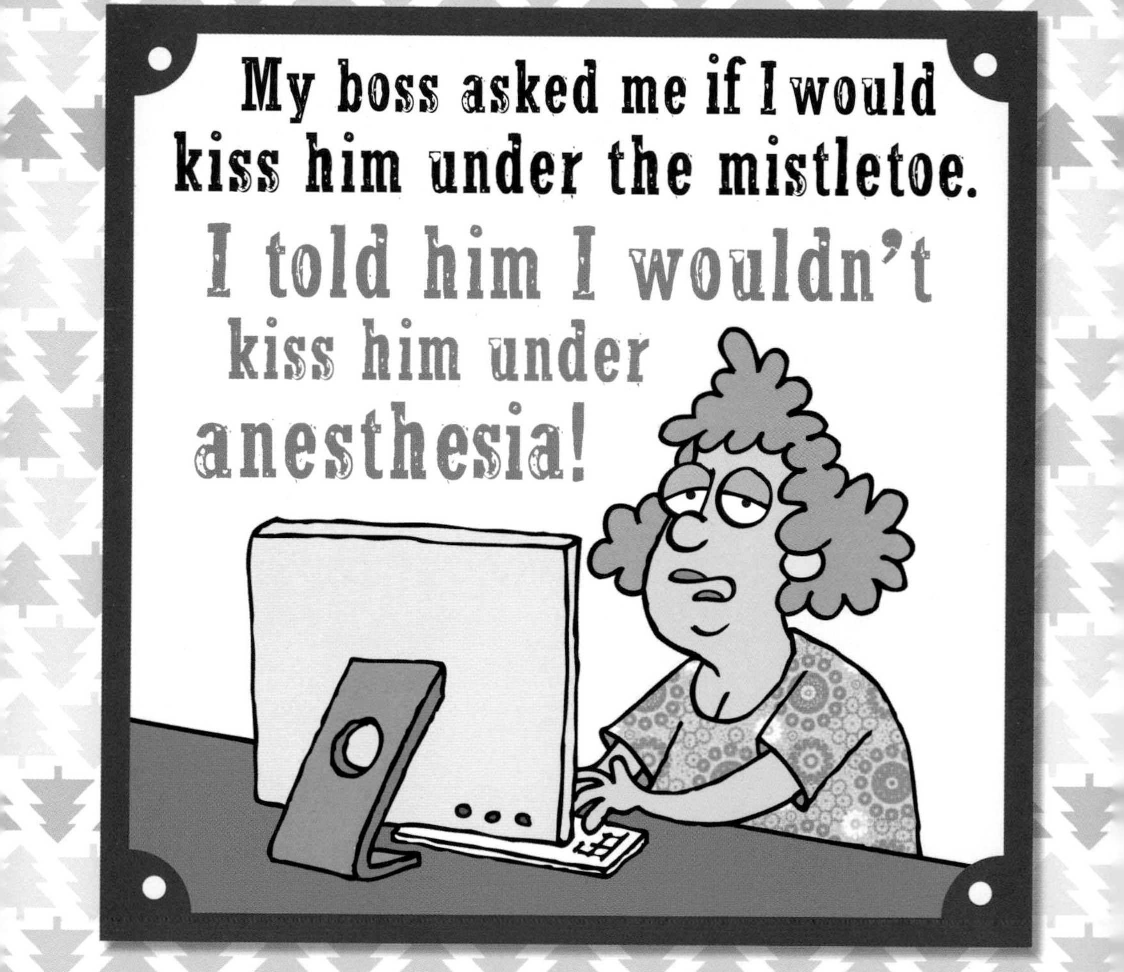
My boss asked me if I would
kiss him under the mistletoe.
I told him I wouldn't
kiss him under
anesthesia!

It's Christmas, of course I've had a tummy tuck...

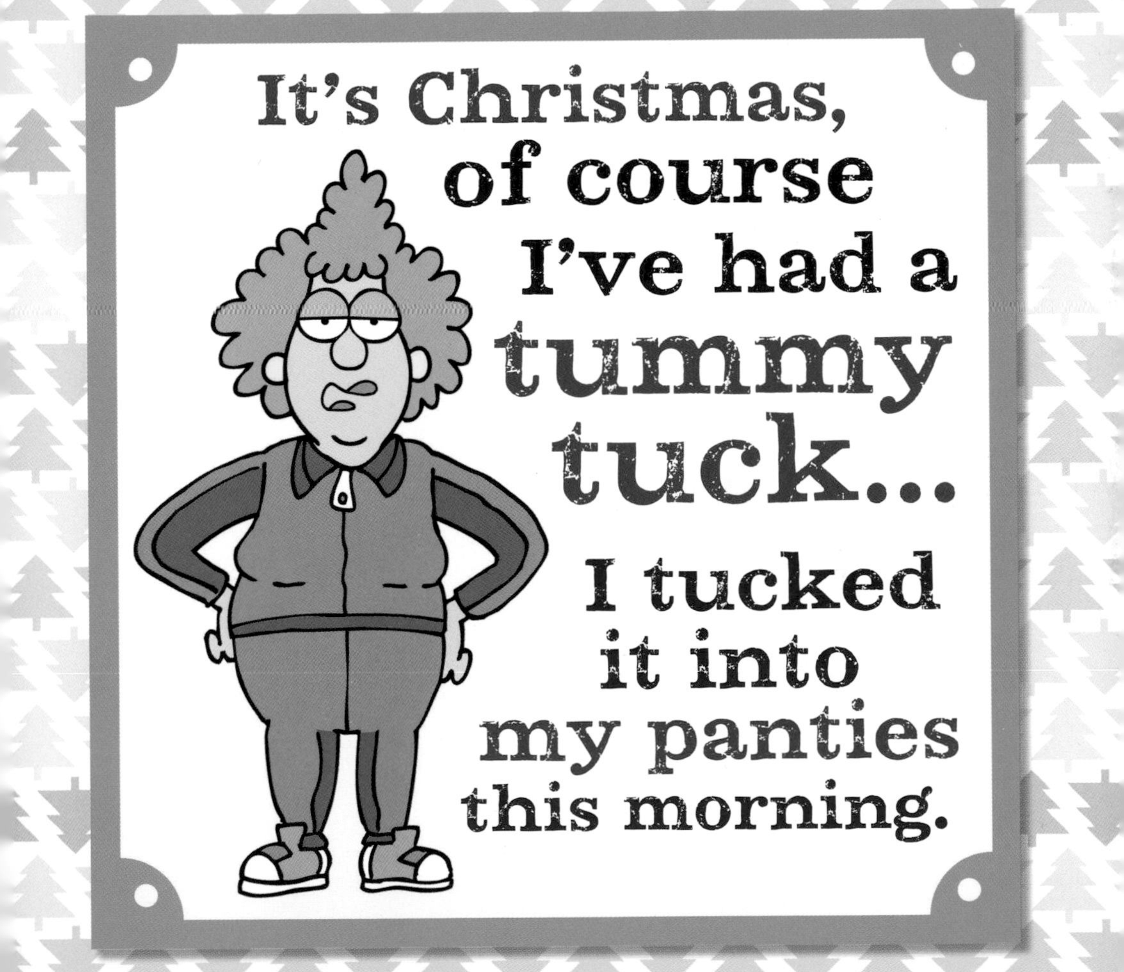

I tucked it into my panties this morning.

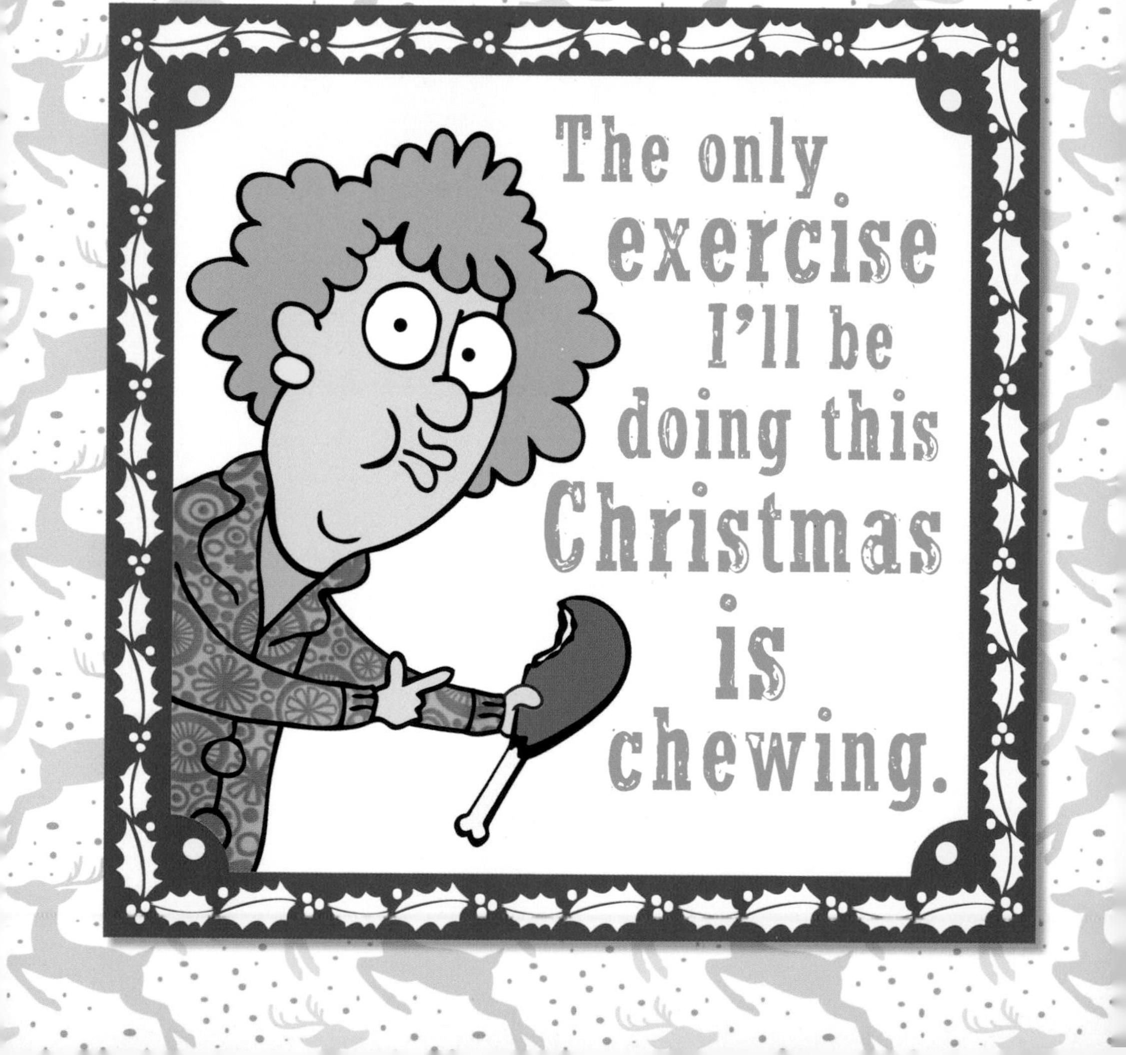
The only exercise I'll be doing this Christmas is chewing.

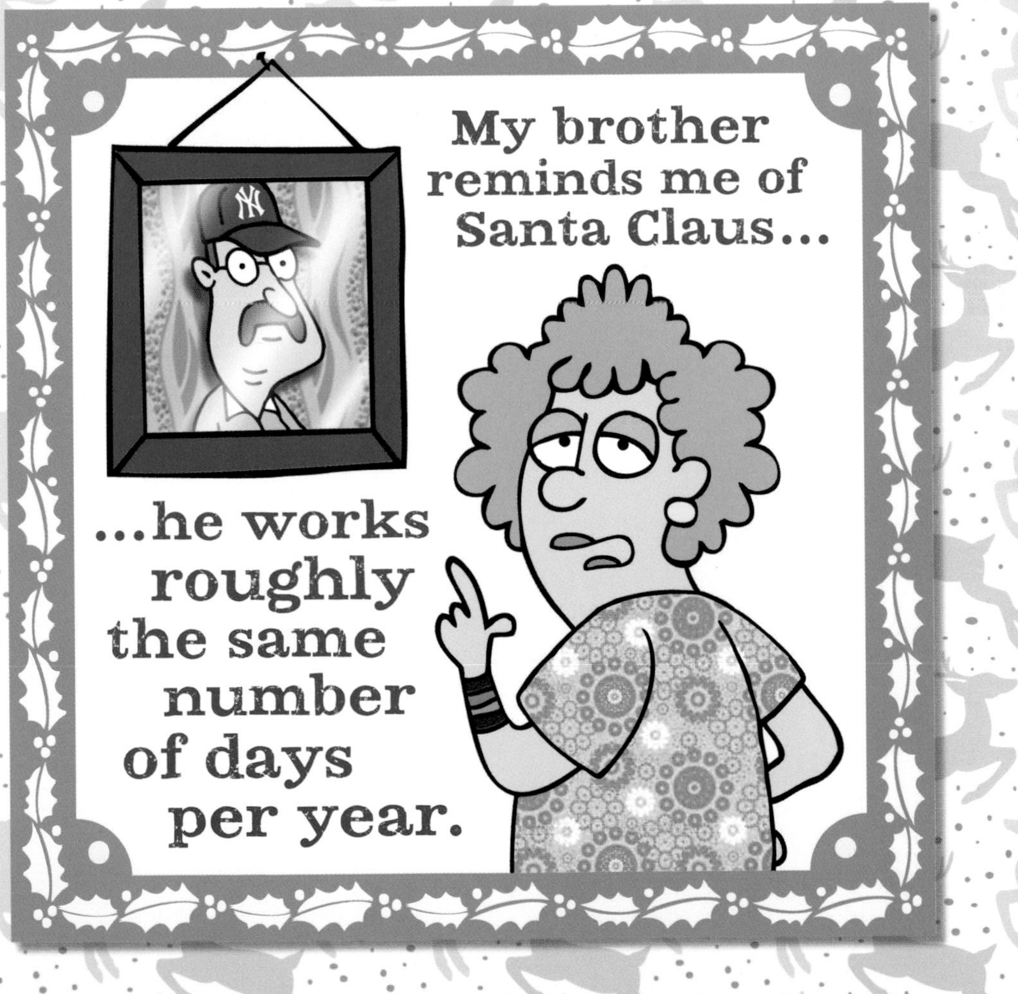
My brother reminds me of Santa Claus...
NY
...he works roughly the same number of days per year.

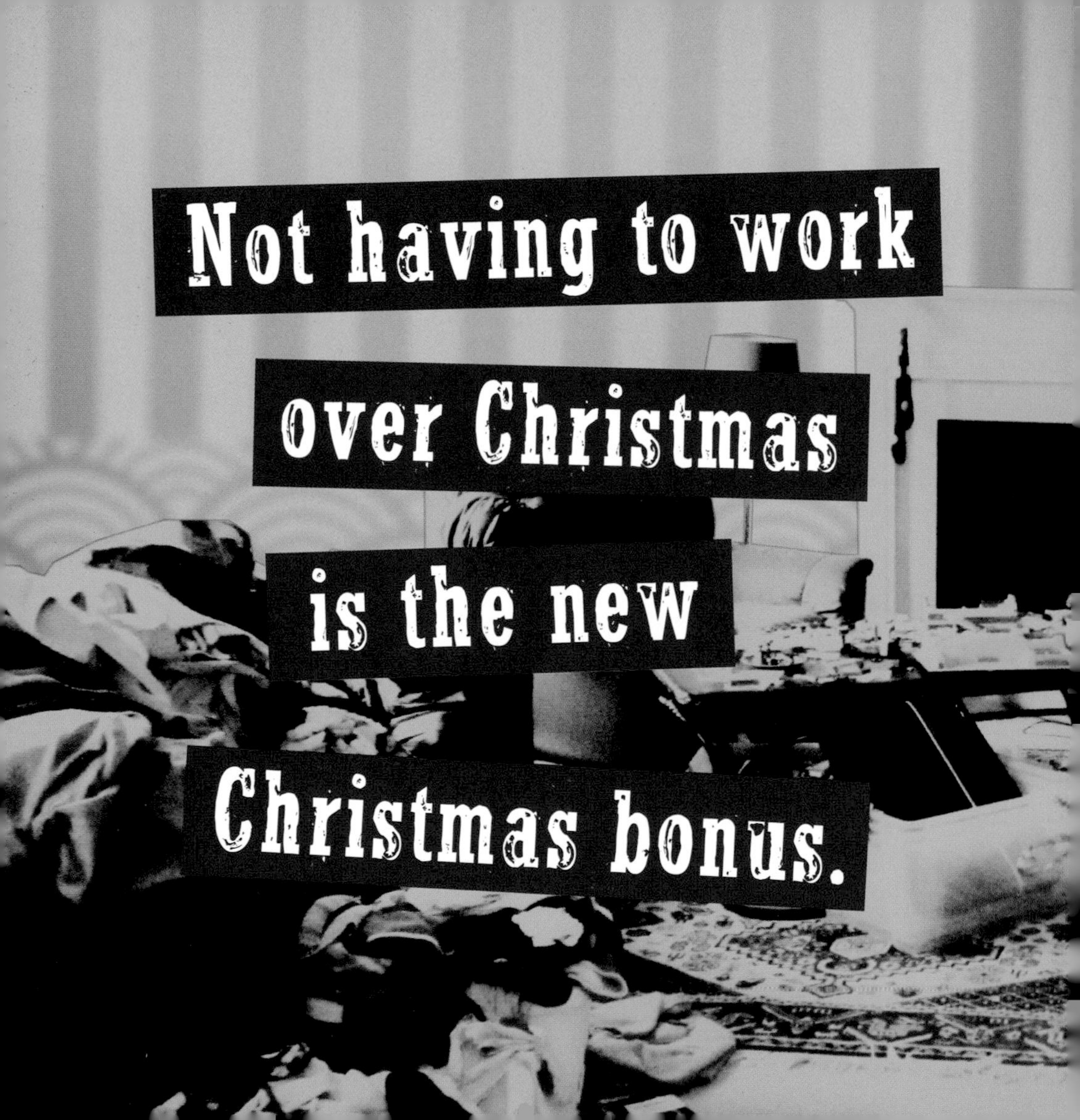
Not having to work
over Christmas
is the new
Christmas bonus.

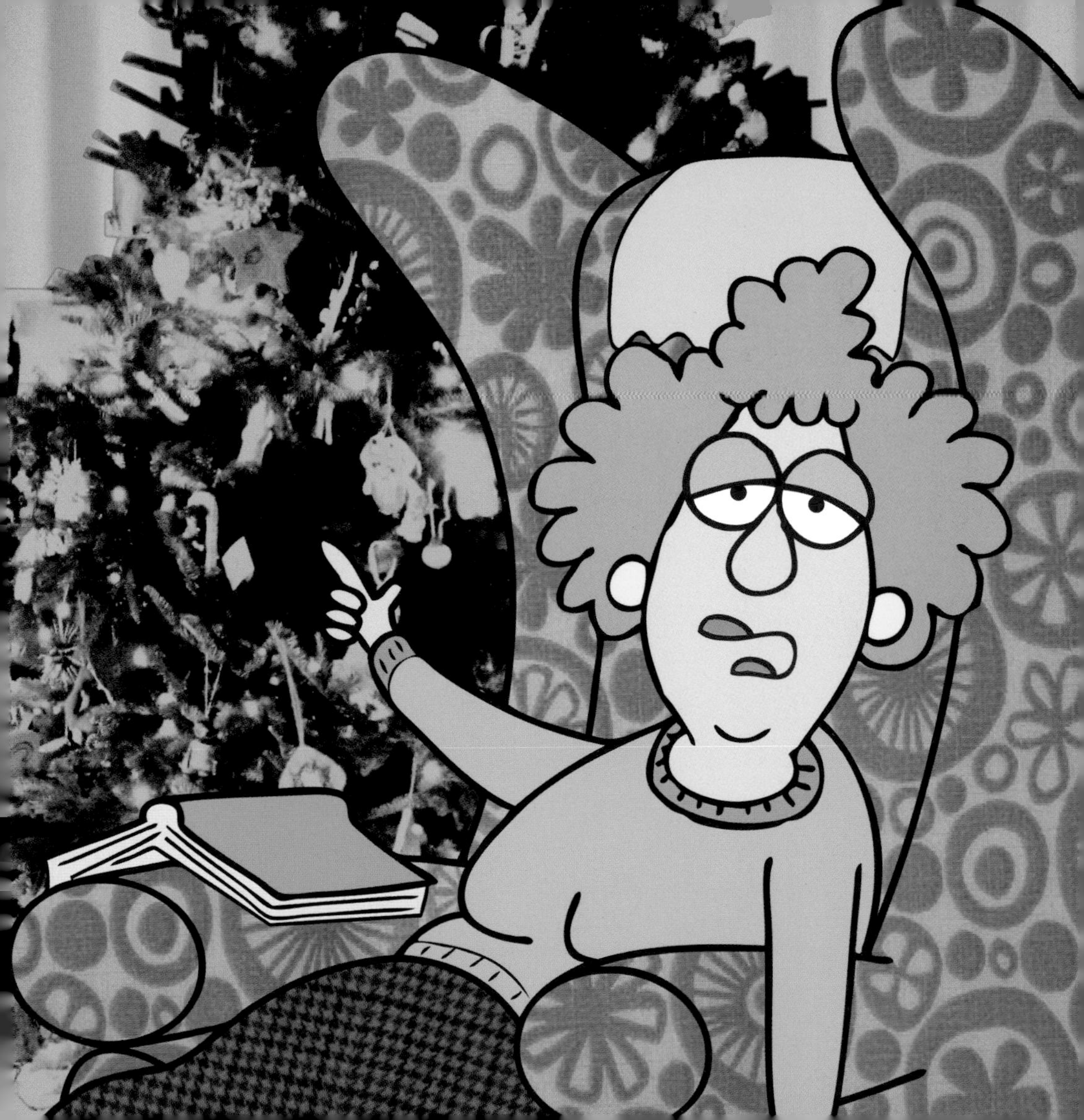

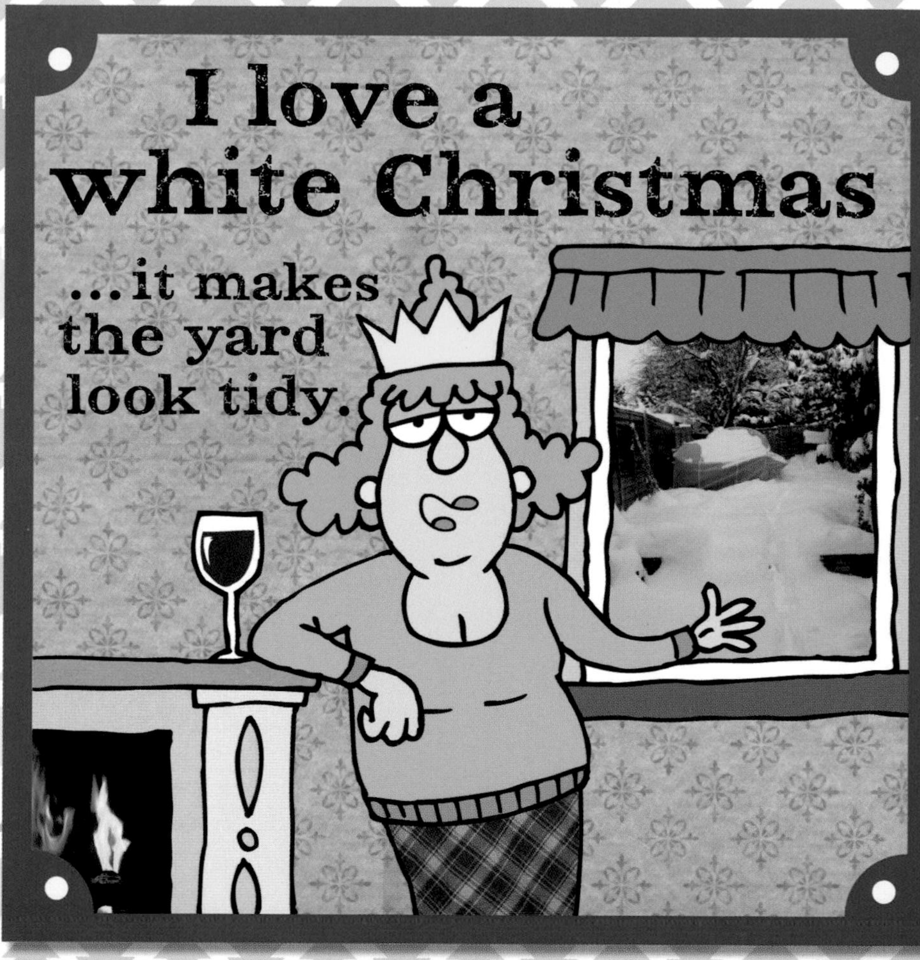
I love a white Christmas
...it makes the yard look tidy.

CHRISTMAS TIP NO.9

I gave the mailman and the paper boy the same tip: "Stay off my freakin' lawn!"

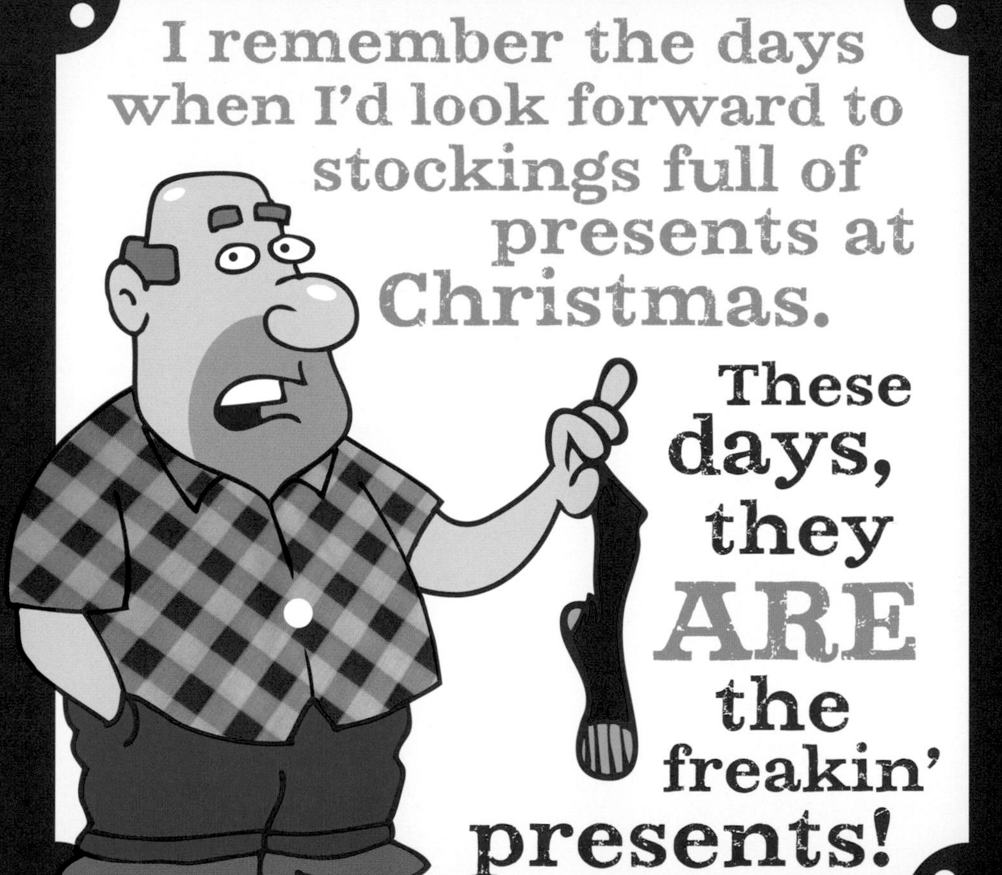
I remember the days when I'd look forward to stockings full of presents at Christmas.
These days, they ARE the freakin' presents!

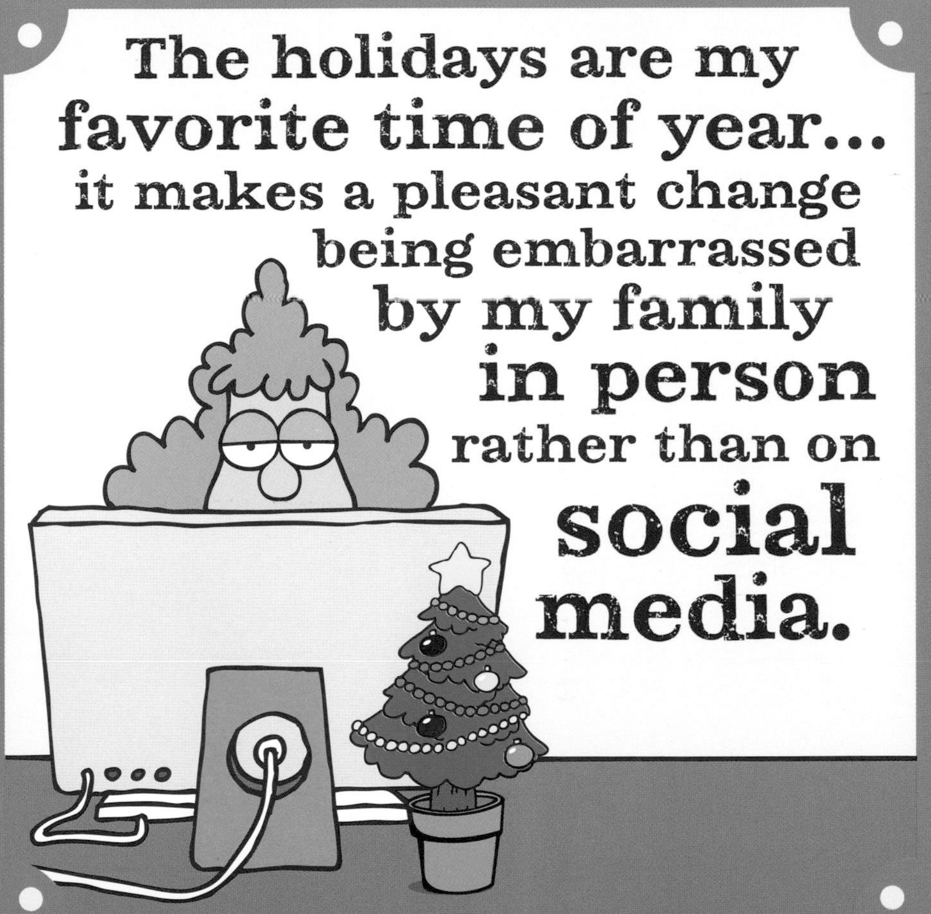
The holidays are my favorite time of year...
it makes a pleasant change being embarrassed by my family in person rather than on social media.

Food and Drink

For some, Christmas might be ALL about the presents or precious time with family, but for me it's about the food and liquor.

'Tis the season to drown in cheese, a large sherry and a pie. You know what the best thing to put in your yams is? Your teeth!

Christmas dinner is my favorite, of course. All those fattening, delicious treats add up, so I've decided to share my Christmas calories rules with you...

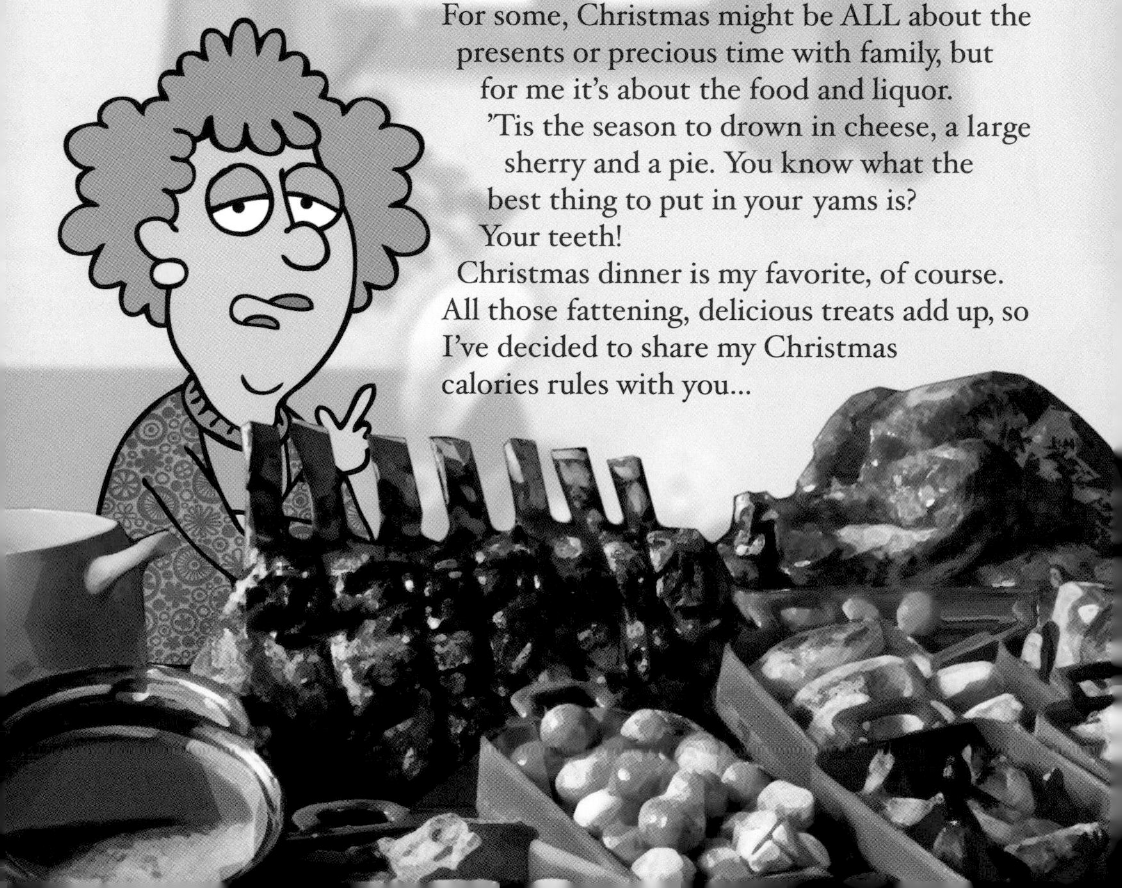

1. If no one sees you eat it, it has no calories.

2. If you eat standing up, it doesn't count!

3. STRESSED is just DESSERTS spelled backwards.

4. If you eat the food off someone else's plate, it doesn't count.

5. When "testing" your food before serving for poison and stuff, it doesn't count.

6. Food used for medicinal purposes has no calories.
This includes: any wine used after visiting in-laws, eggnog used after shopping, cheesecake used after a present wrapping session and Häagen-Dazs ice cream for anytime in between.

7. Food eaten at Christmas parties has no calories, courtesy of Santa.

8. Cookie pieces contain no calories because the process of breakage causes calorie leakage.

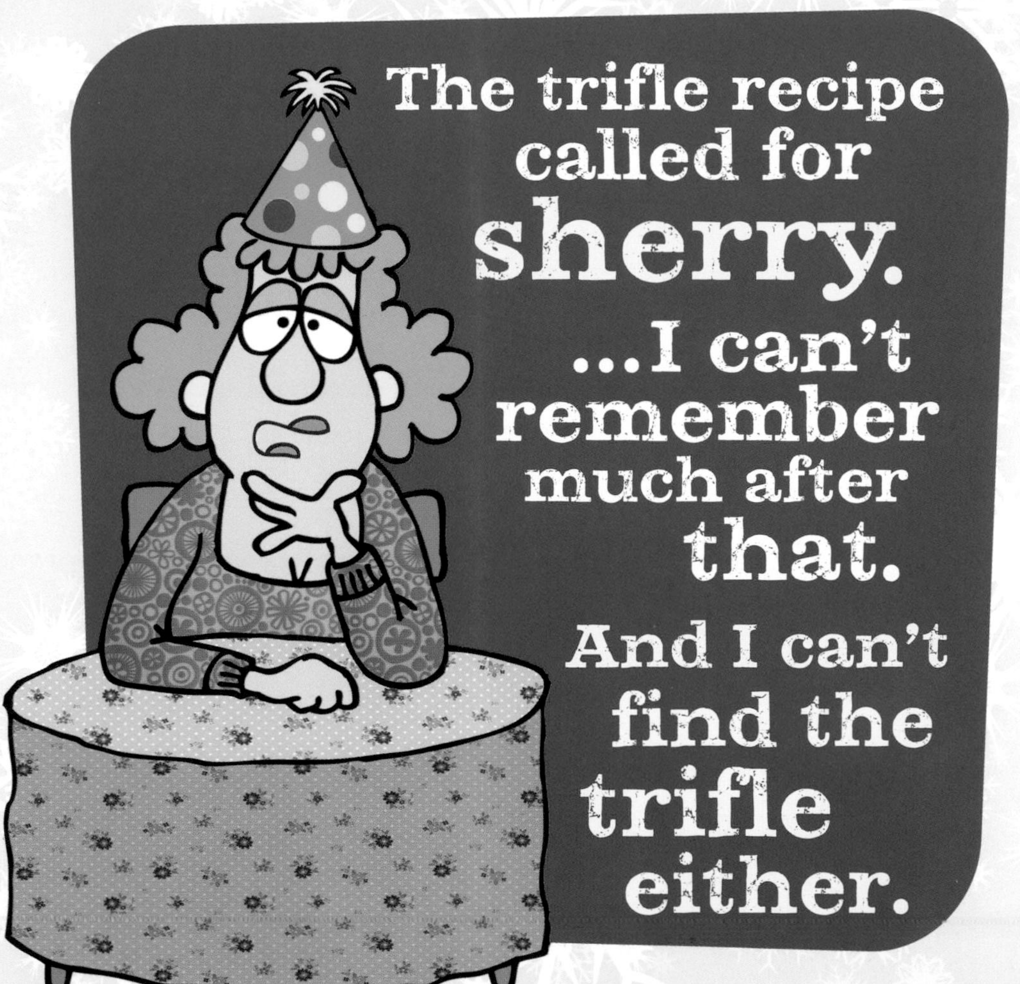

The trifle recipe called for **sherry.**

...I can't remember much after **that.**

And I can't find the **trifle** either.

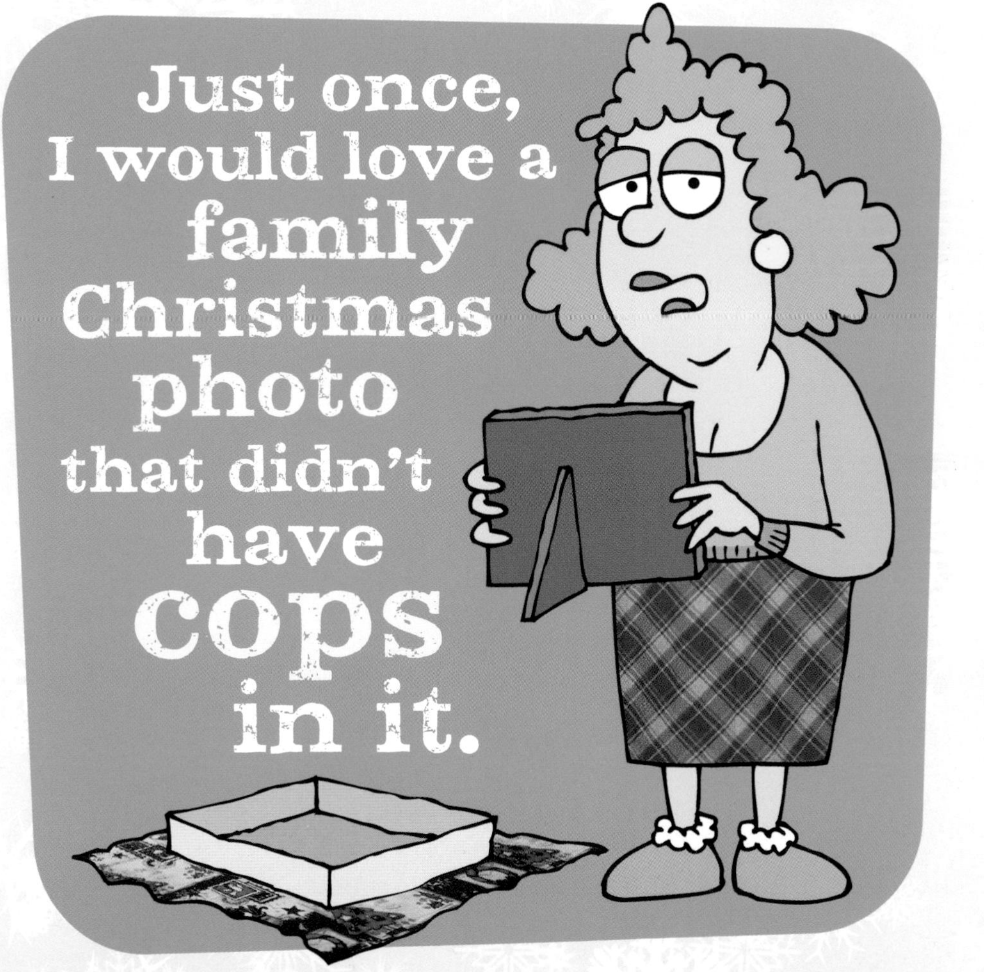
Just once,
I would love a
family
Christmas
photo
that didn't
have
cops
in it.

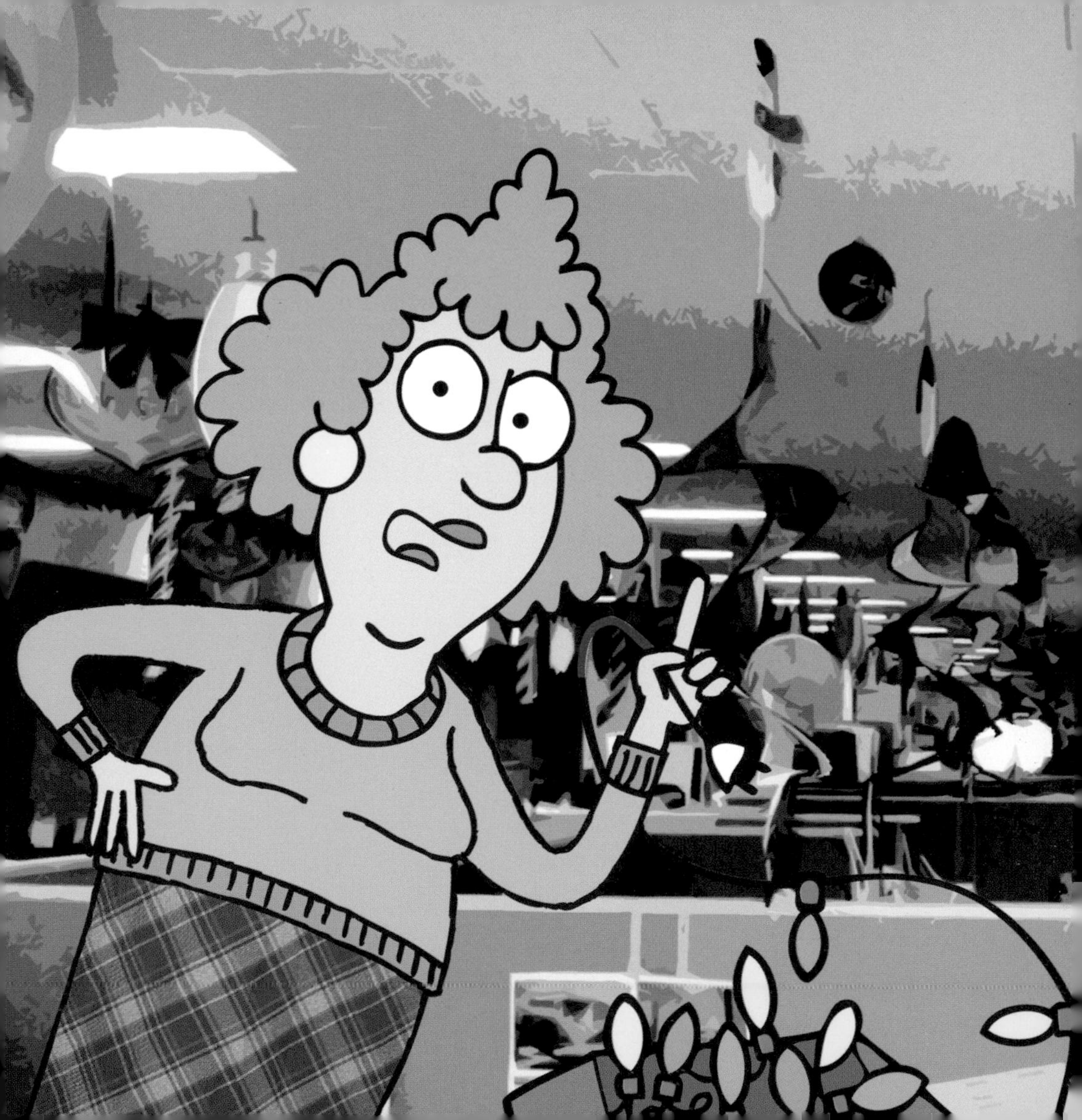

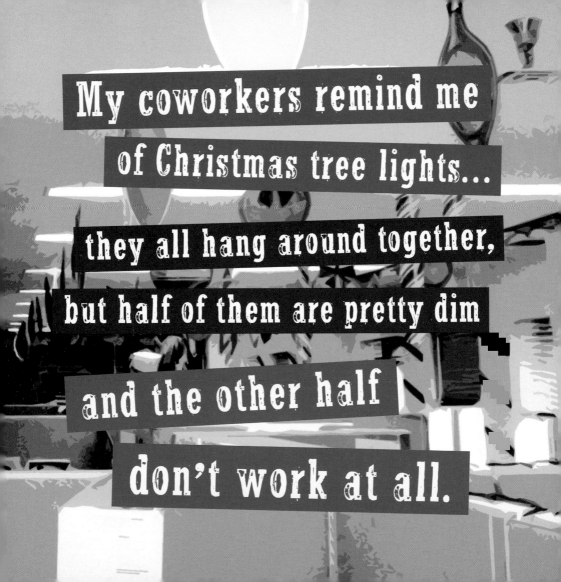

My coworkers remind me of Christmas tree lights... they all hang around together, but half of them are pretty dim and the other half don't work at all.

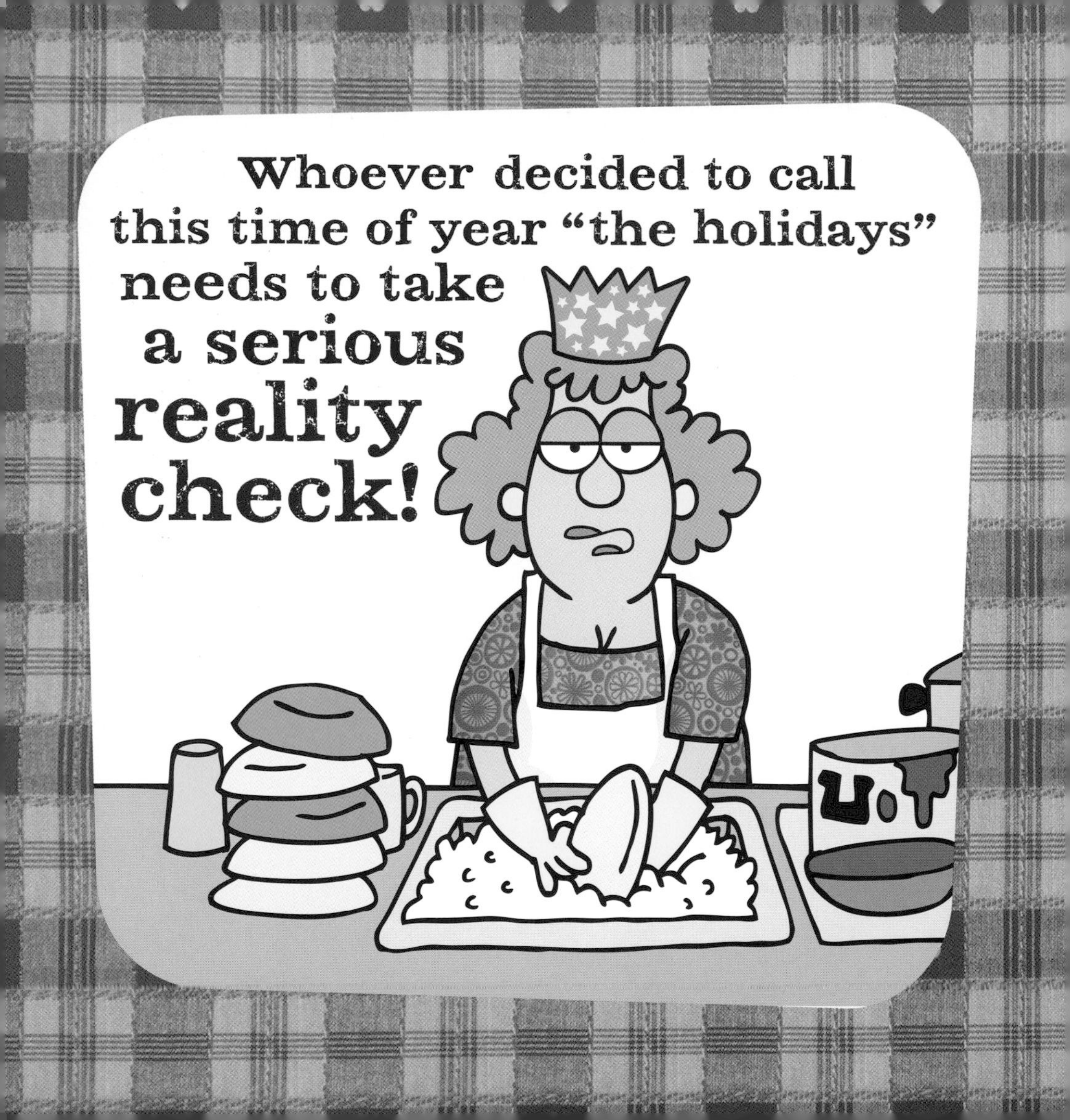
Whoever decided to call this time of year "the holidays" needs to take a serious reality check!

AUNTY ACID'S MESSAGE TO CAROL SINGERS

You can knock all you want,
And sing for an hour or more.
I'll just turn my TV up,
And not answer the freakin' door!

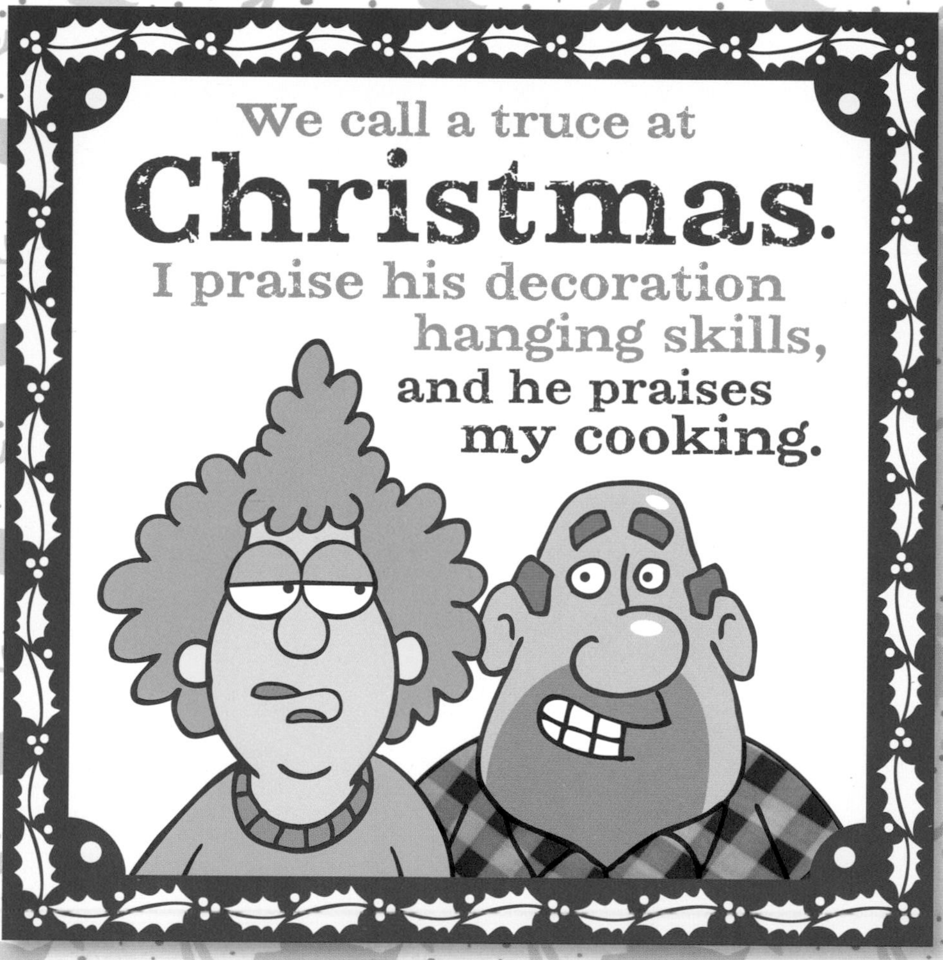
We call a truce at
Christmas.
I praise his decoration
hanging skills,
and he praises
my cooking.

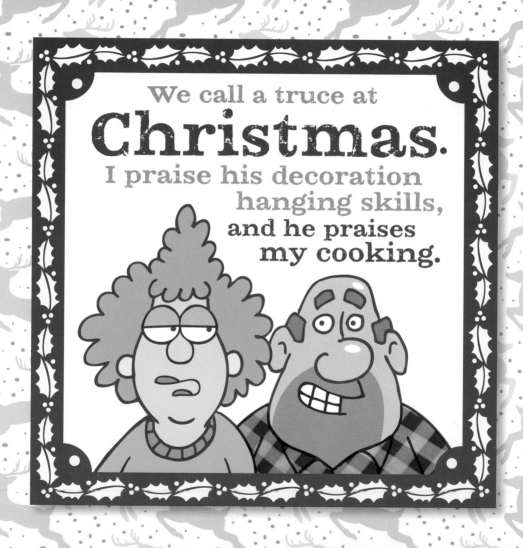

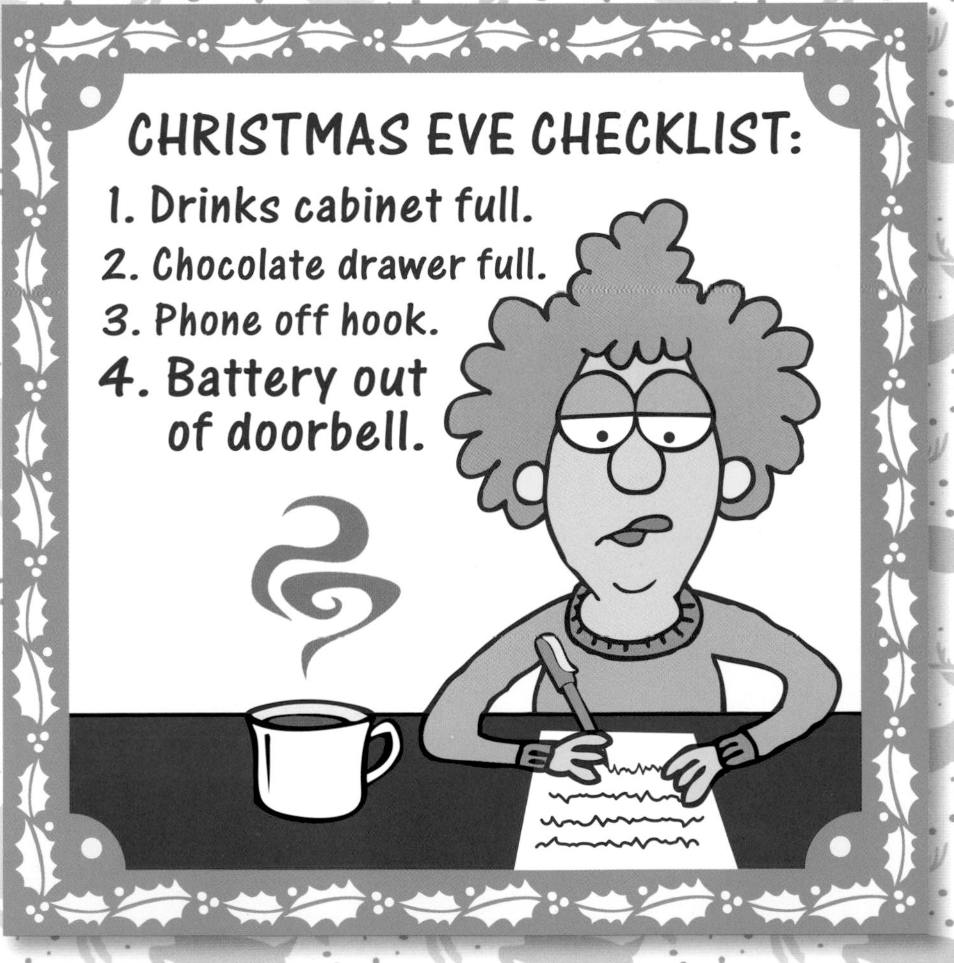
CHRISTMAS EVE CHECKLIST:
1. Drinks cabinet full.
2. Chocolate drawer full.
3. Phone off hook.
4. Battery out of doorbell.

When I serve **Walt's mother** Christmas dinner, I always ask the same question...
is anything ok?

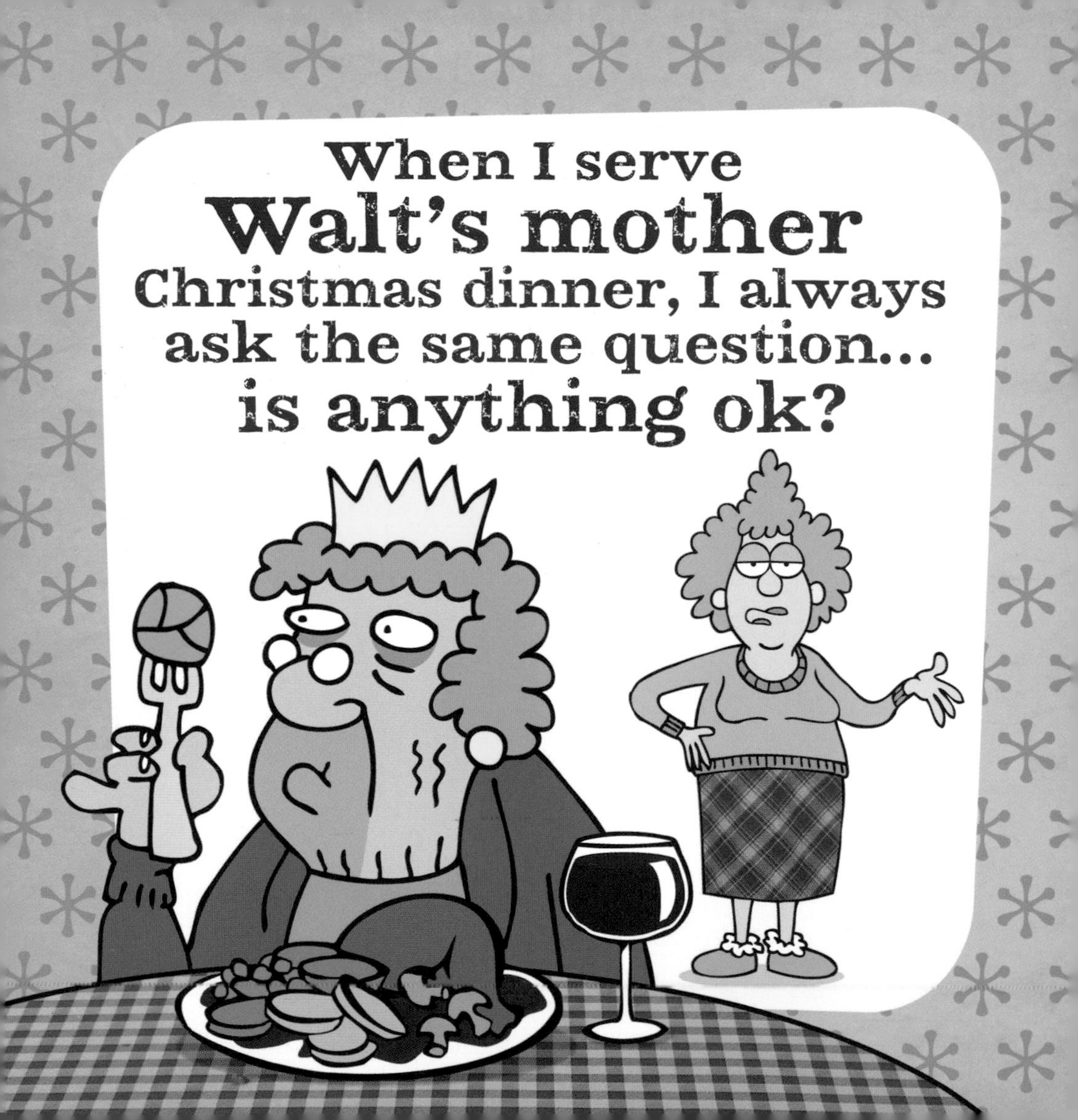

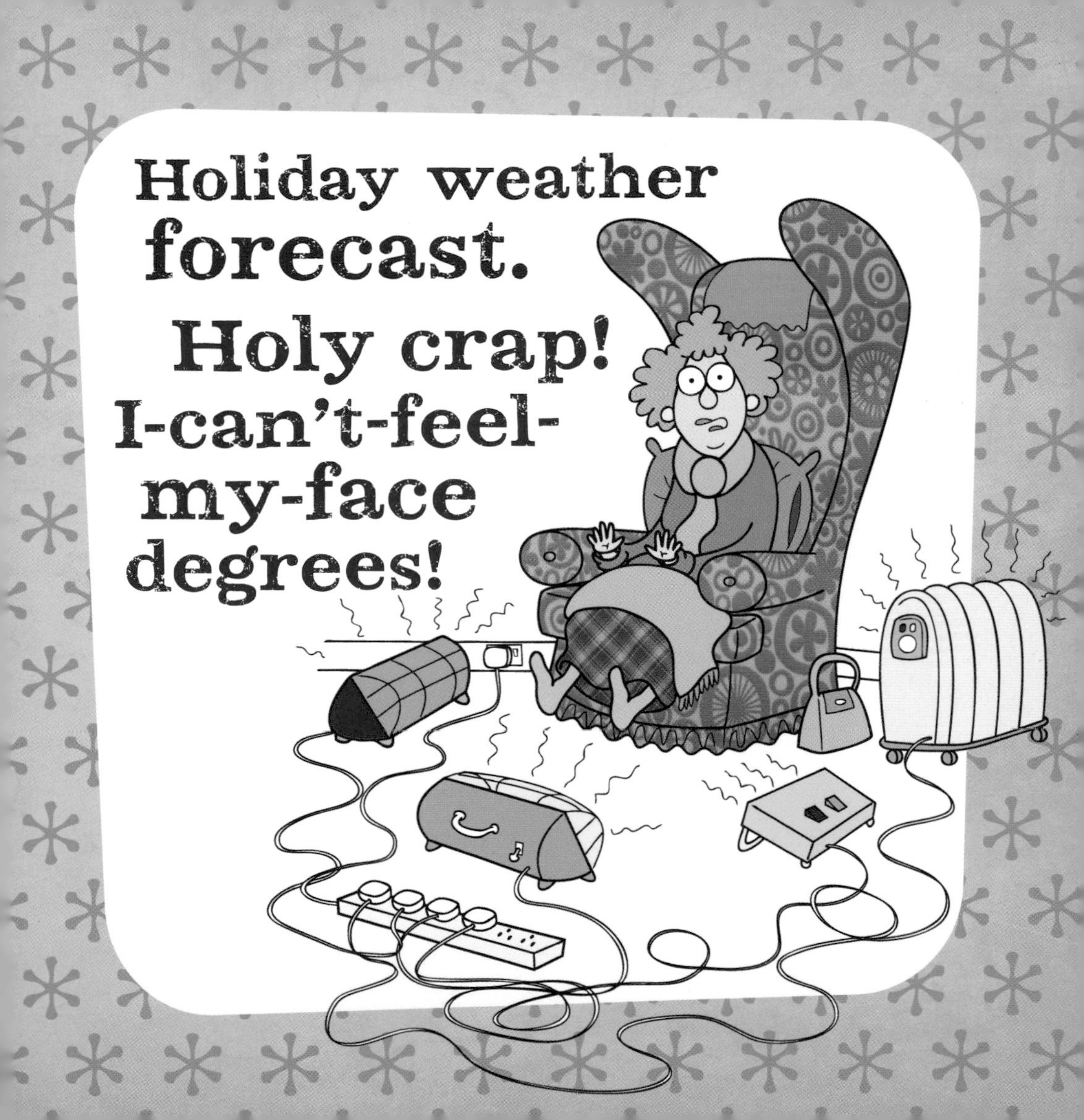
Holiday weather forecast.
Holy crap! I-can't-feel-my-face degrees!

Relatives

I was reading an article the other day entitled, "How to Deal with Difficult Relatives Over Christmas," but they left out my favorite tip, *"Don't answer the freakin' door!"*

Walt has his mother coming over for Christmas lunch, so for a more relaxed family meal this year, I've decided to stuff the turkey . . . with Prozac!

Joking aside, I do love sharing a drink with the family over the holiday season; it definitely makes a change from drinking *because of them*.

I believe there's nothing more magical than a dysfunctional family trying to function for the holiday; it sure makes me believe in Christmas miracles. So I'm wishing you a season full of strong family bonding and even stronger gin, because as my old friend Ben Franklin said, *"Guests, like fish, begin to smell after three days."*

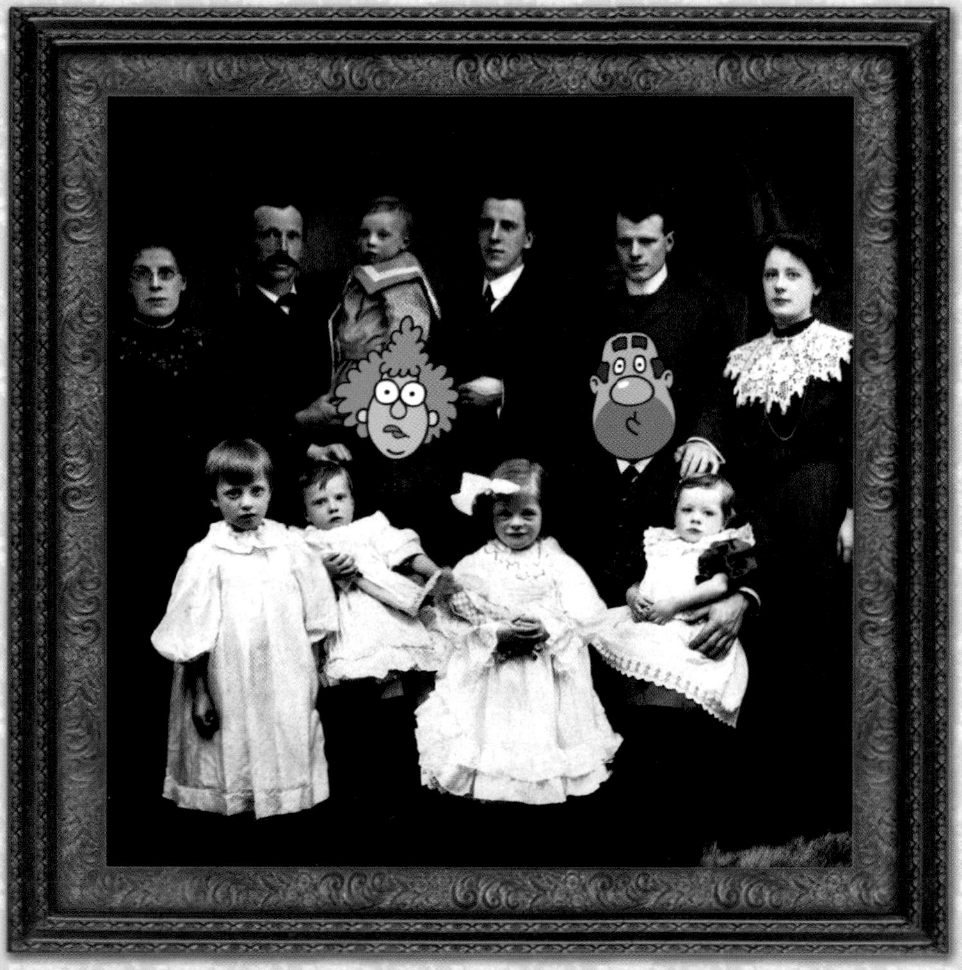

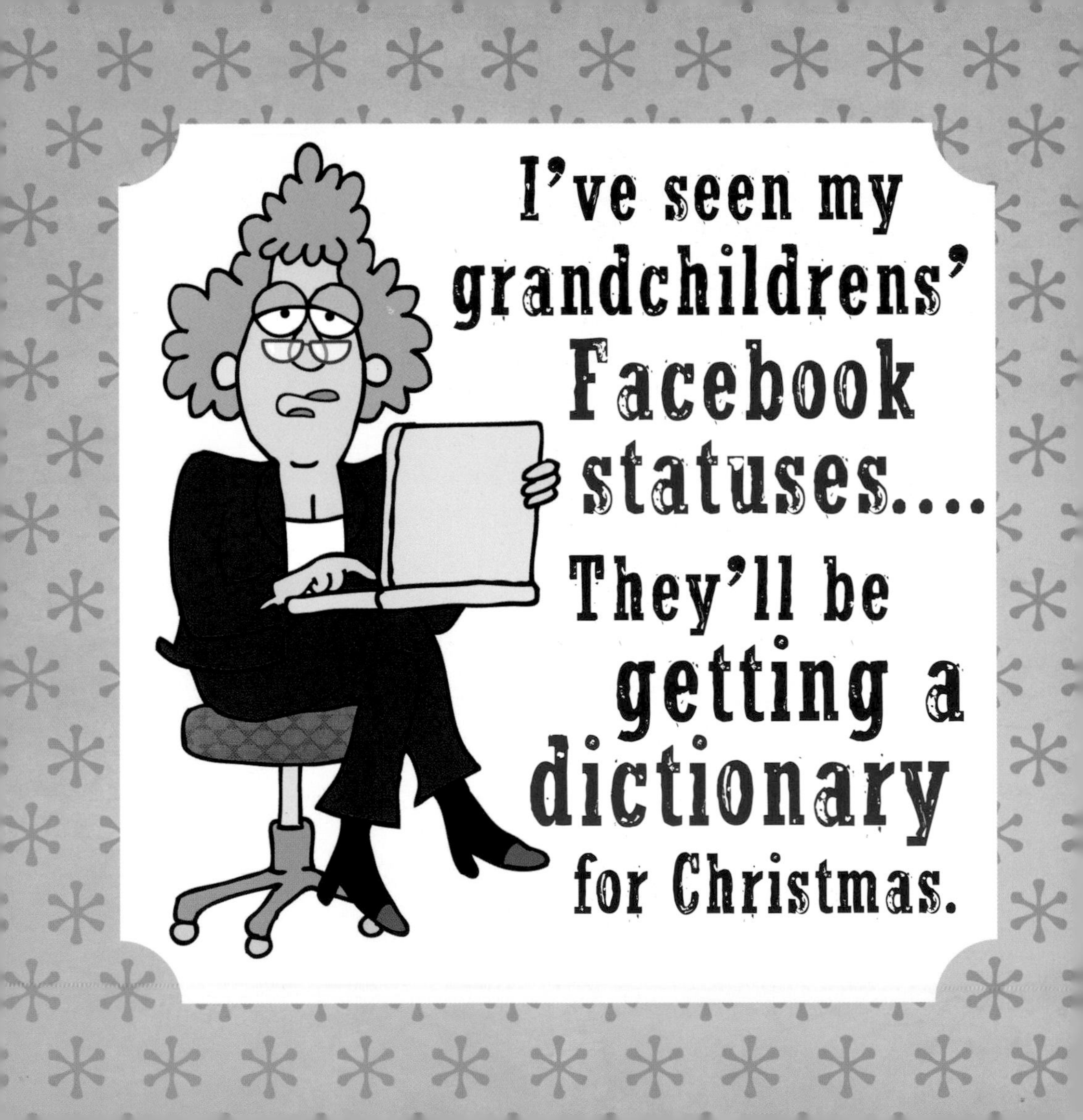

I've seen my grandchildrens' Facebook statuses.... They'll be getting a dictionary for Christmas.

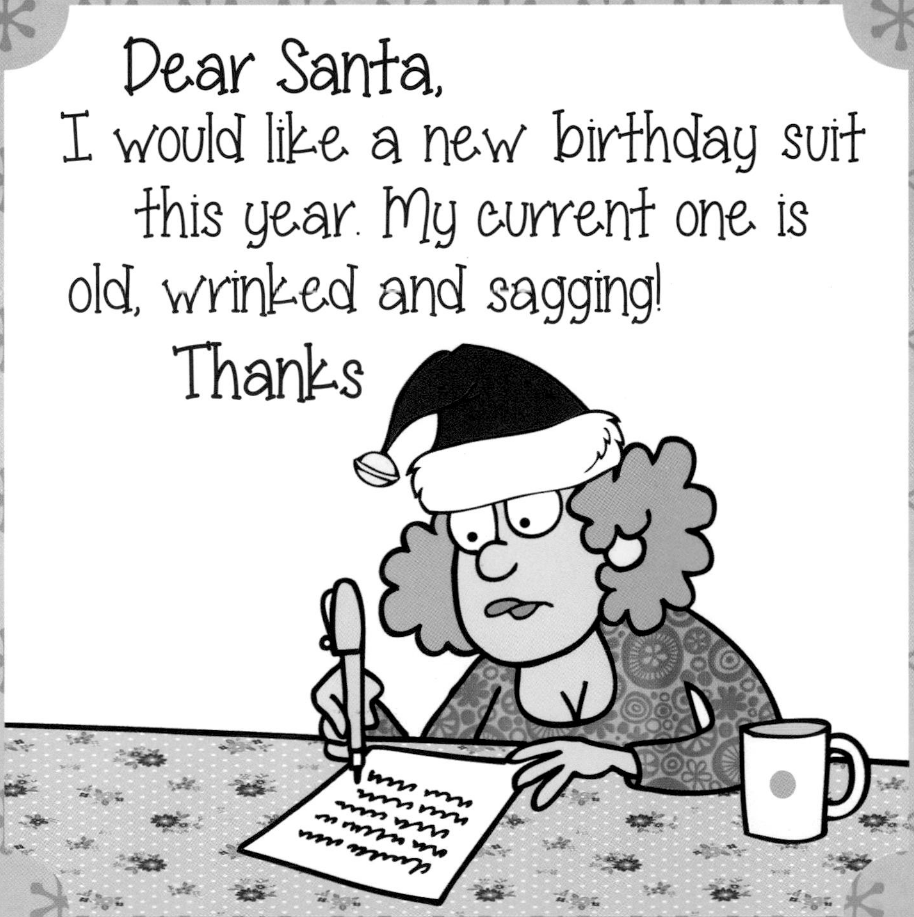
Dear Santa,
I would like a new birthday suit this year. My current one is old, wrinked and sagging!
Thanks

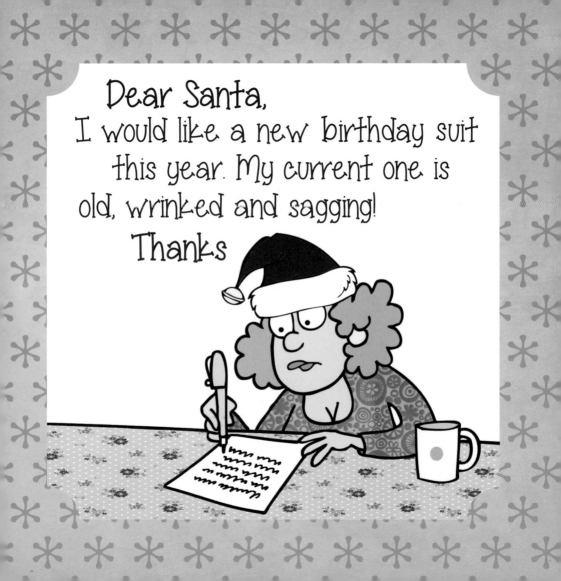

If you're going to be a **smart ass** this Christmas, first make sure you're **smart...** otherwise you're just **an ass.**

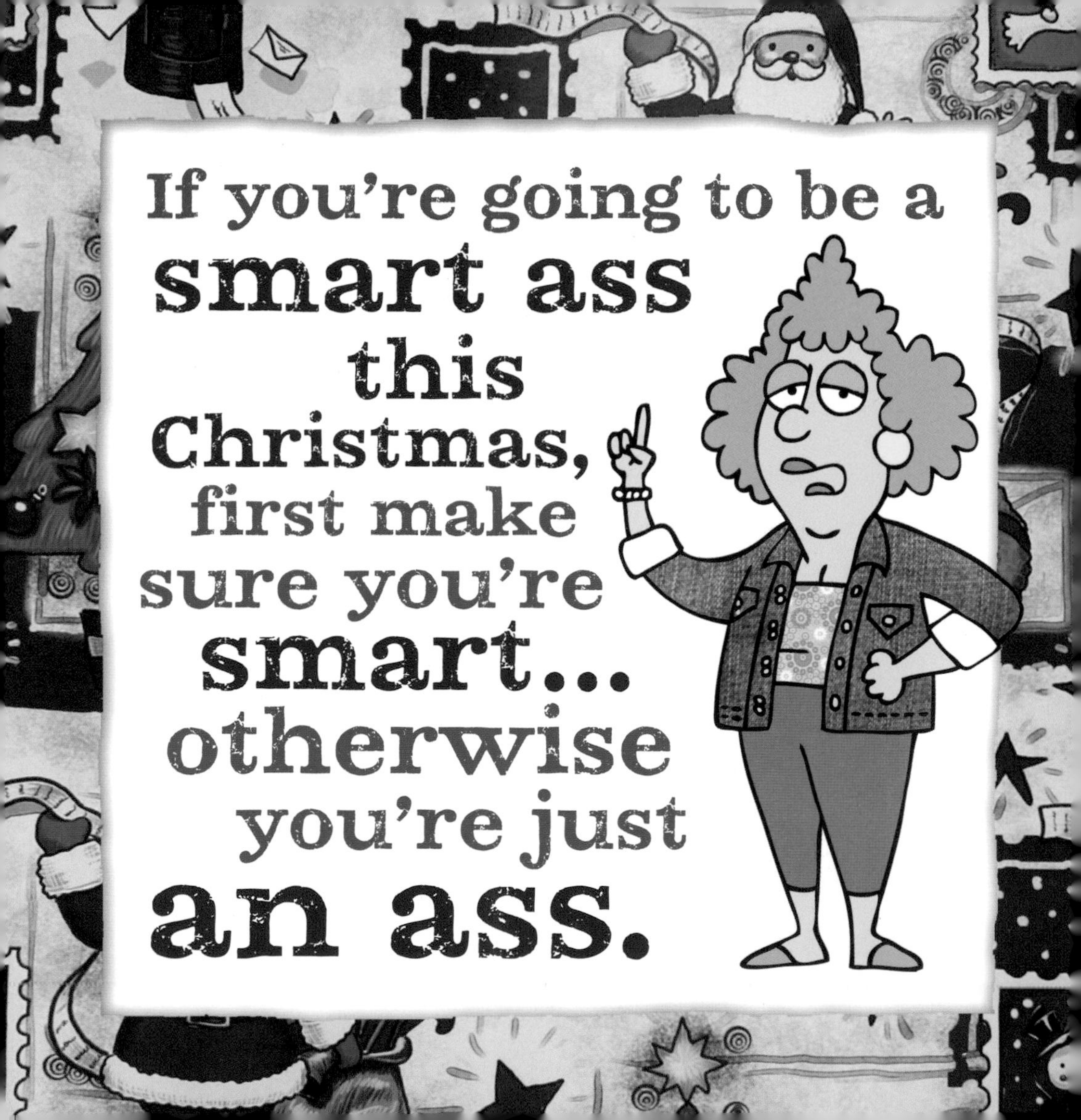

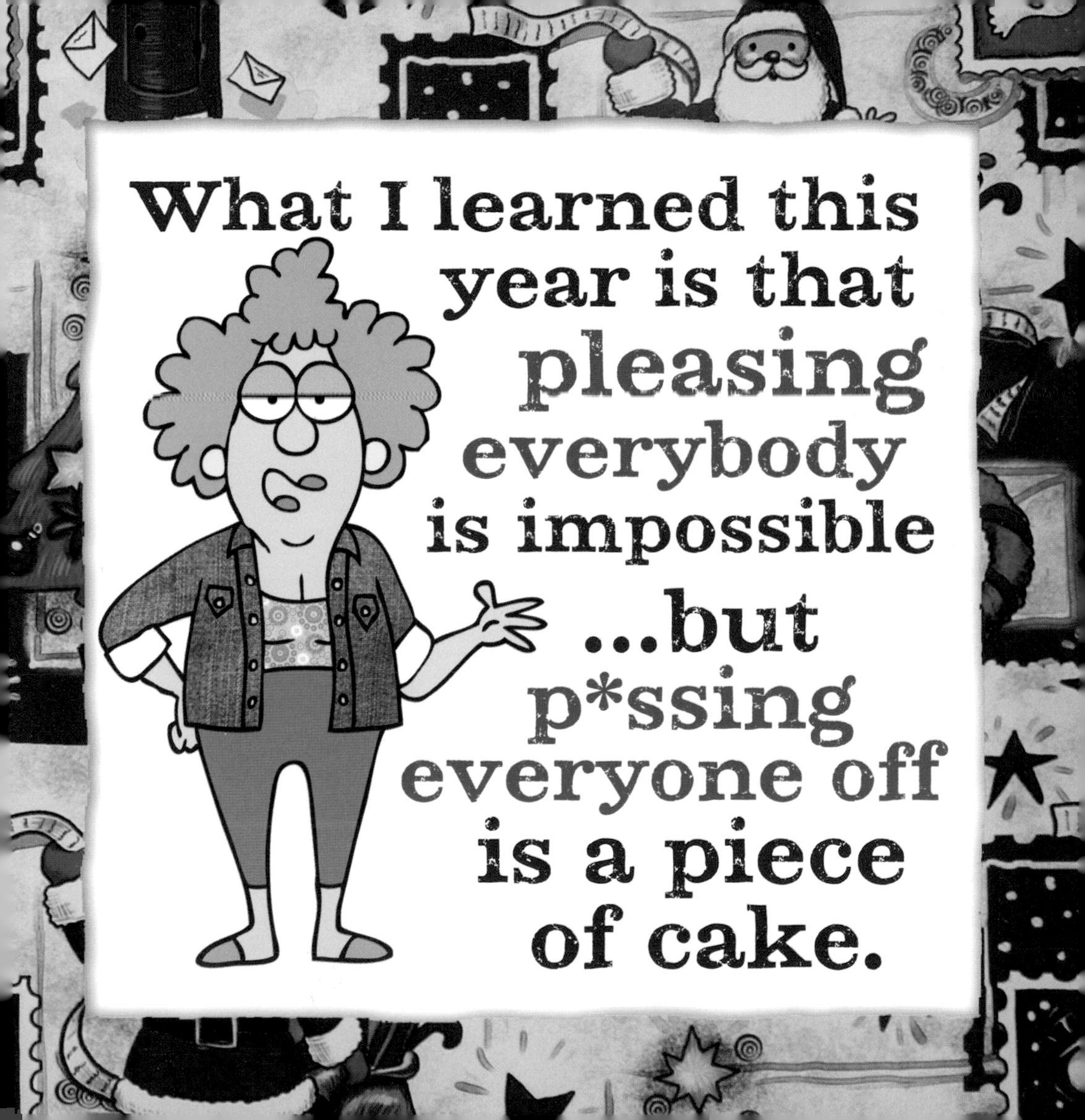
What I learned this year is that pleasing everybody is impossible
...but p*ssing everyone off is a piece of cake.

The worst thing about **Christmas** office parties is looking for a new job the day after.

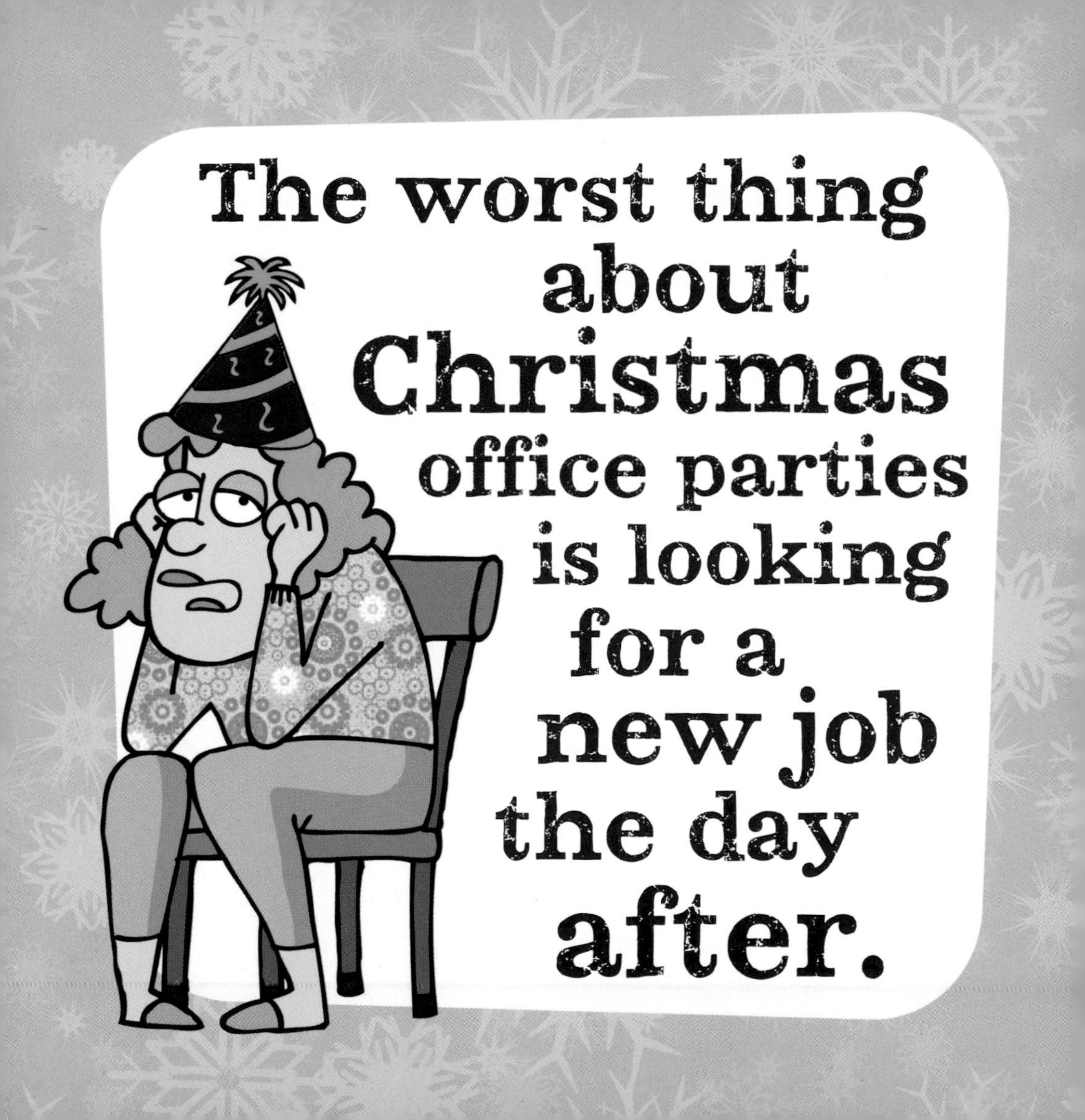

Santa has the right idea... visit people once a freakin' year and get out as quick as you can.

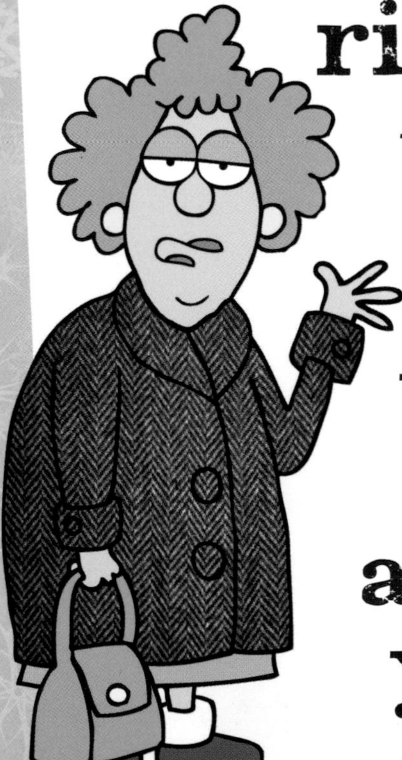

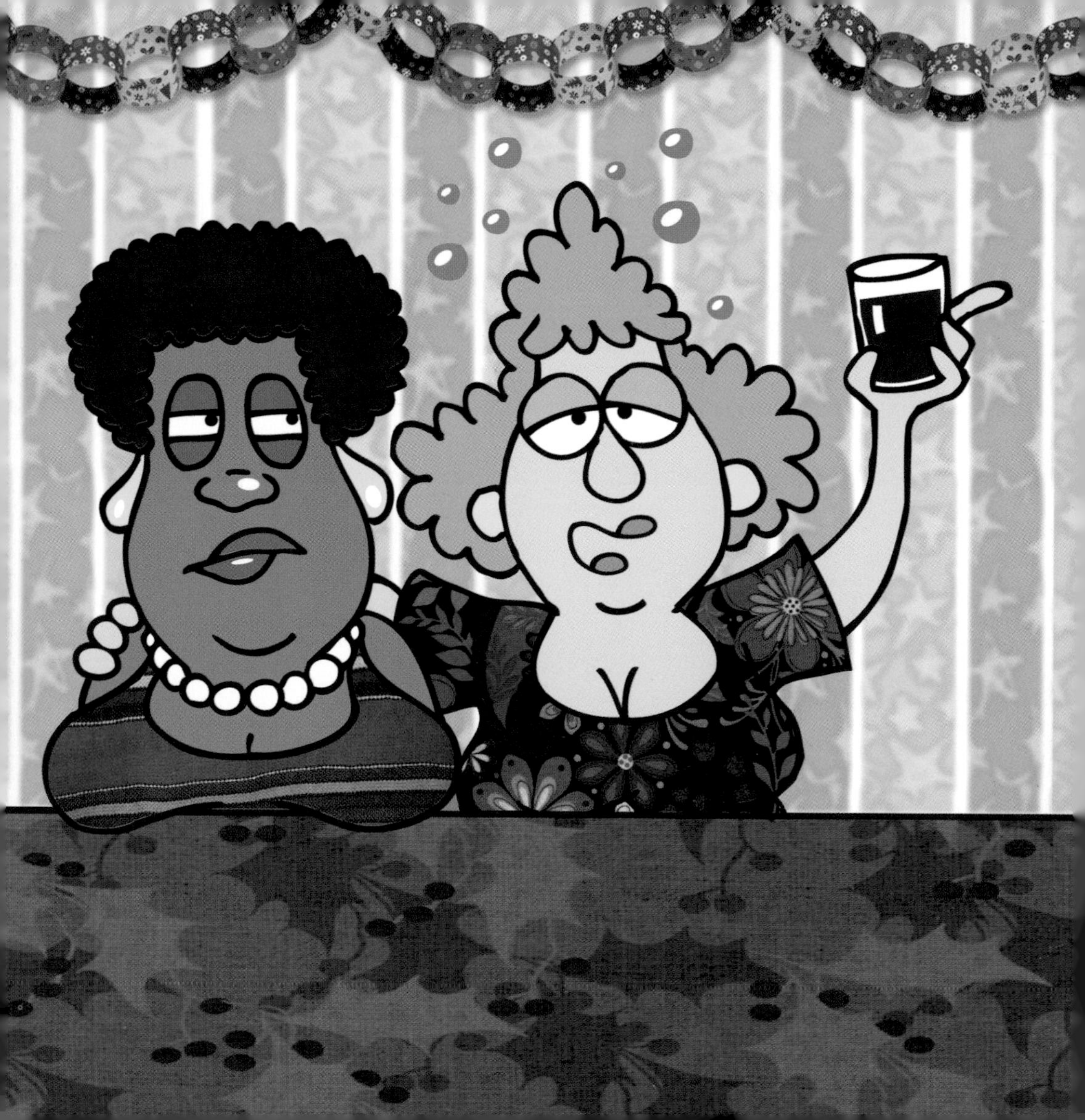

If I didn't drink
at Christmas,
how would my
friends know
I loved them at
two in the morning?

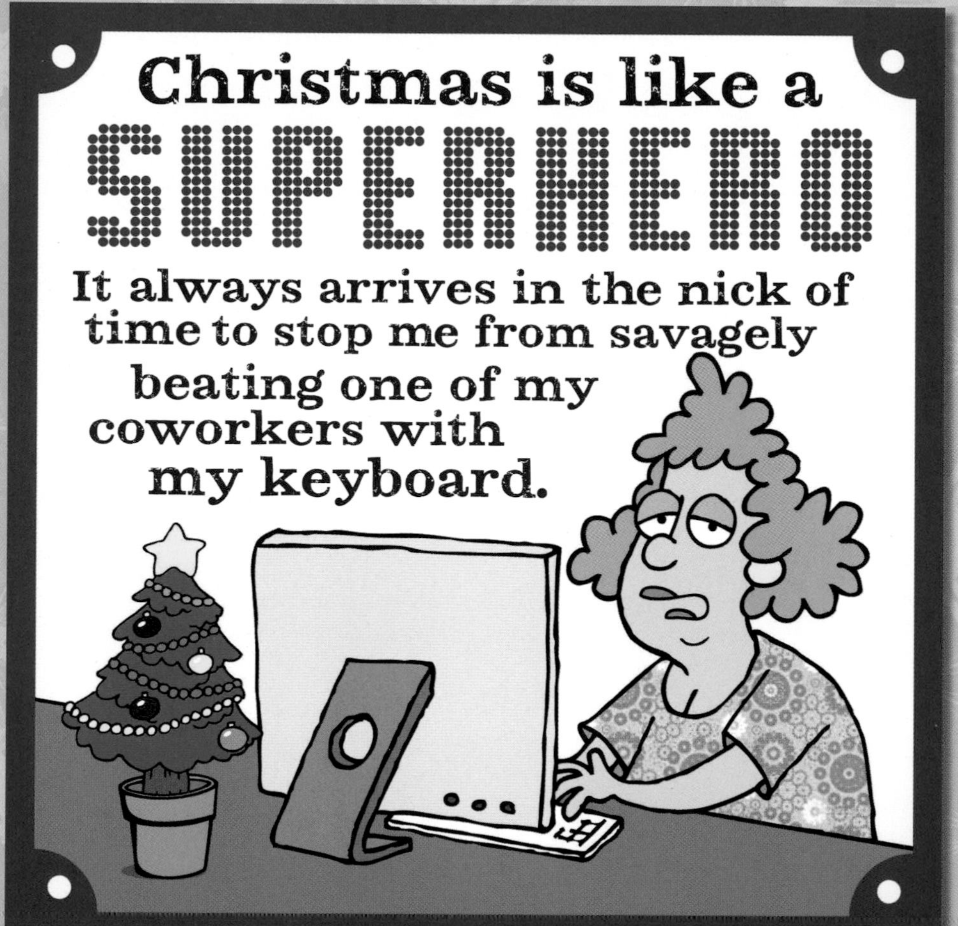
Christmas is like a
SUPERHERO
It always arrives in the nick of time to stop me from savagely beating one of my coworkers with my keyboard.

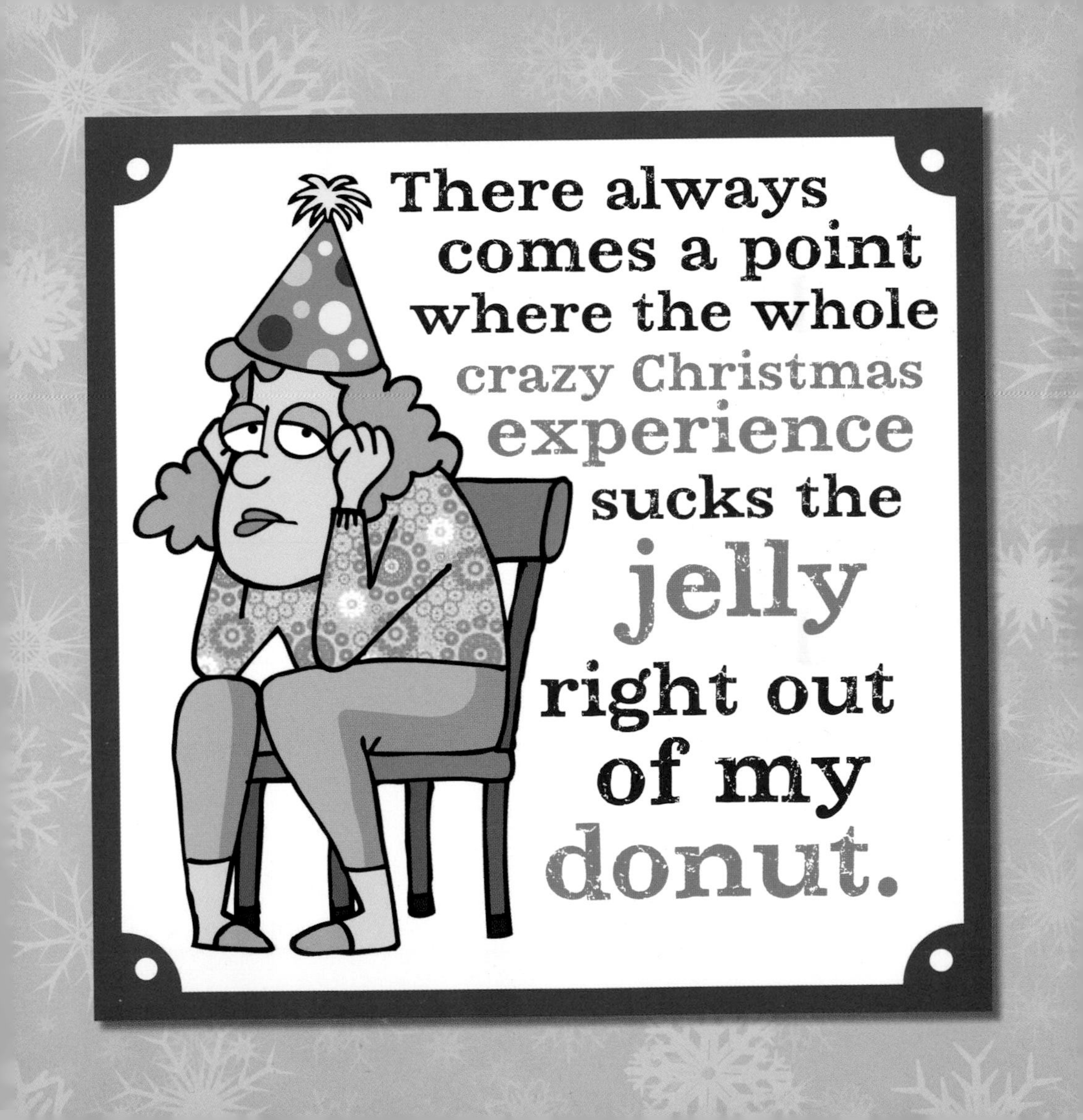

There always comes a point where the whole crazy Christmas experience sucks the jelly right out of my donut.

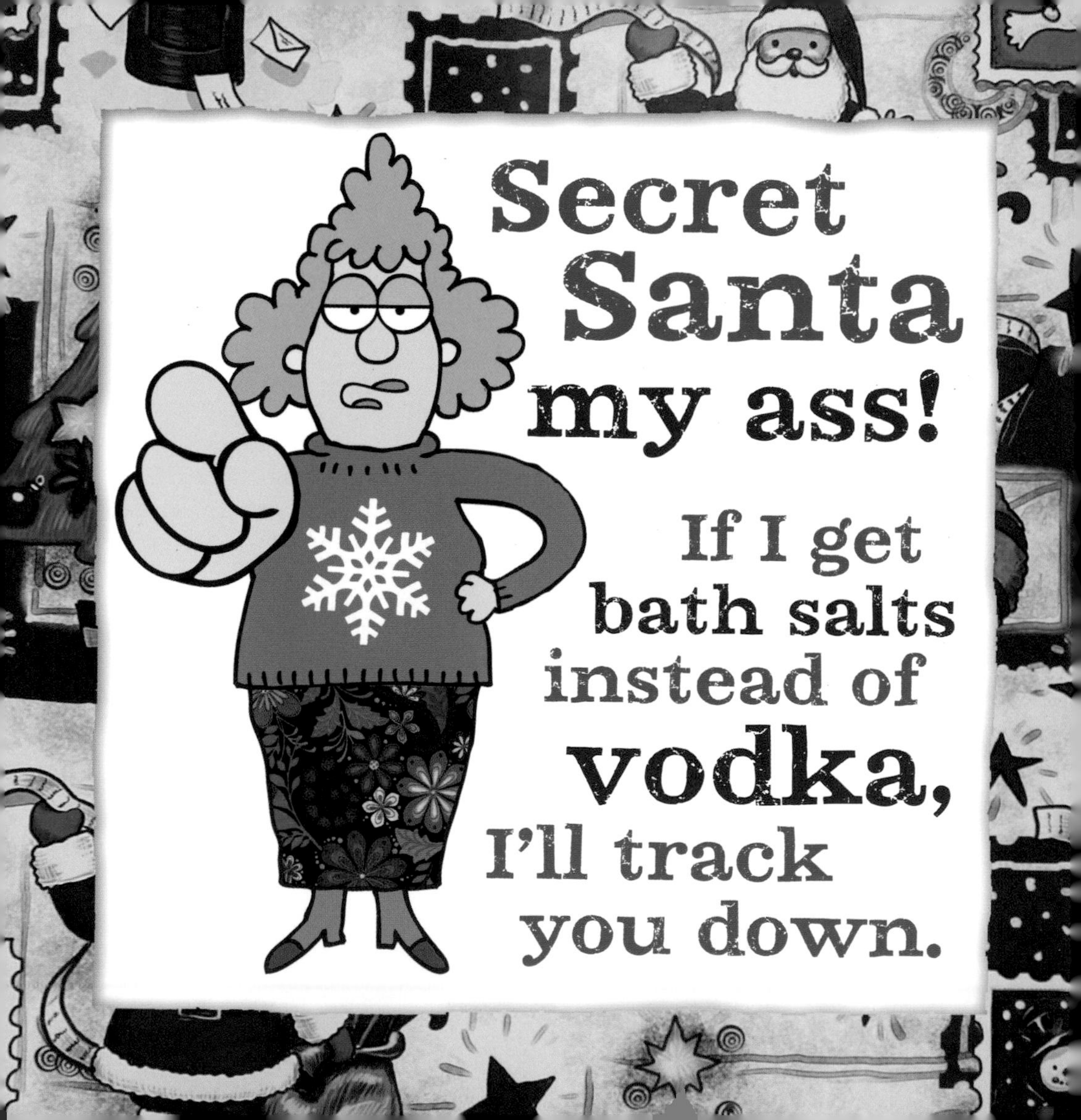

Secret
Santa
my ass!

If I get
bath salts
instead of
vodka,
I'll track
you down.

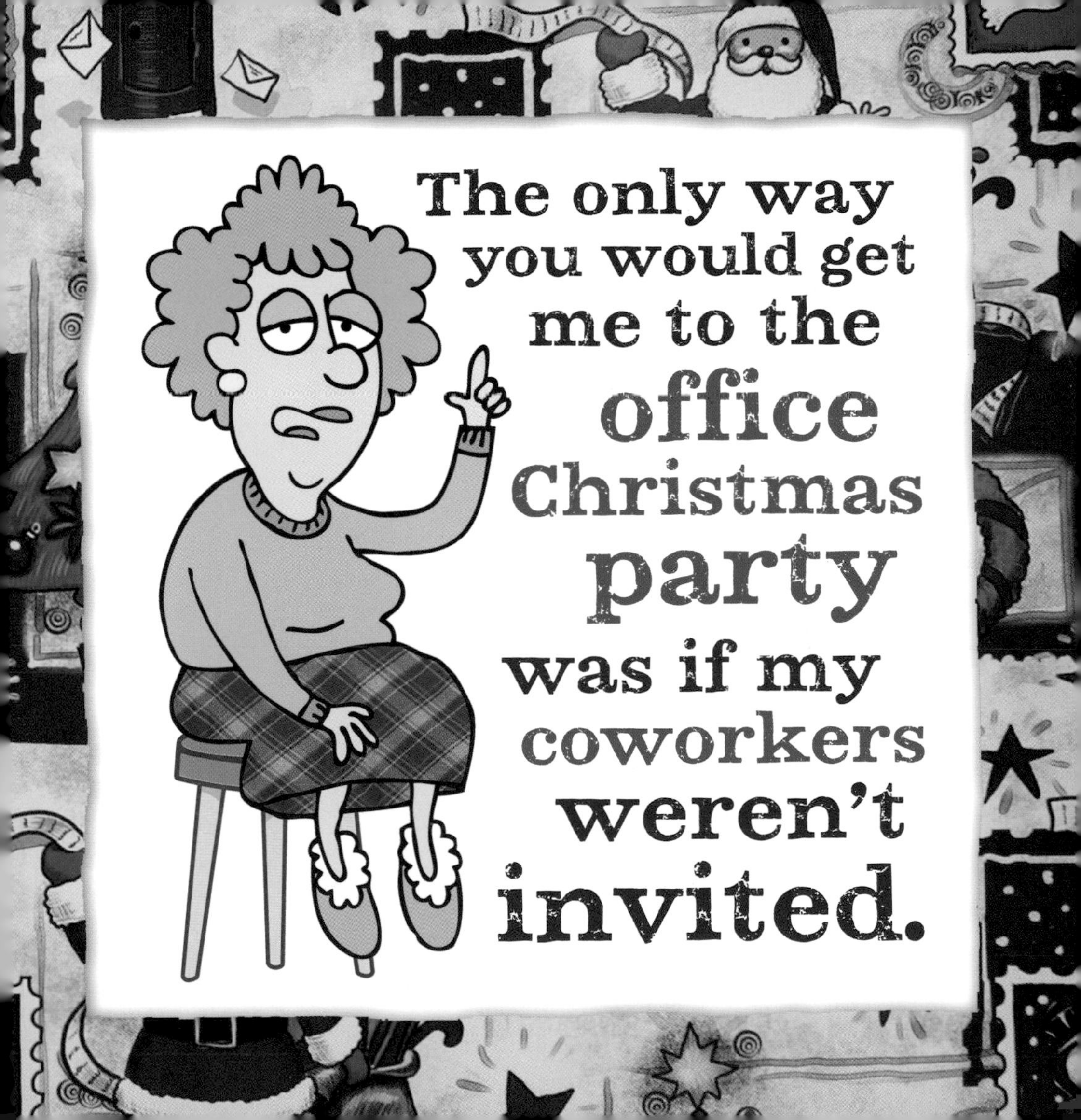

The only way you would get me to the **office Christmas party** was if my coworkers weren't invited.

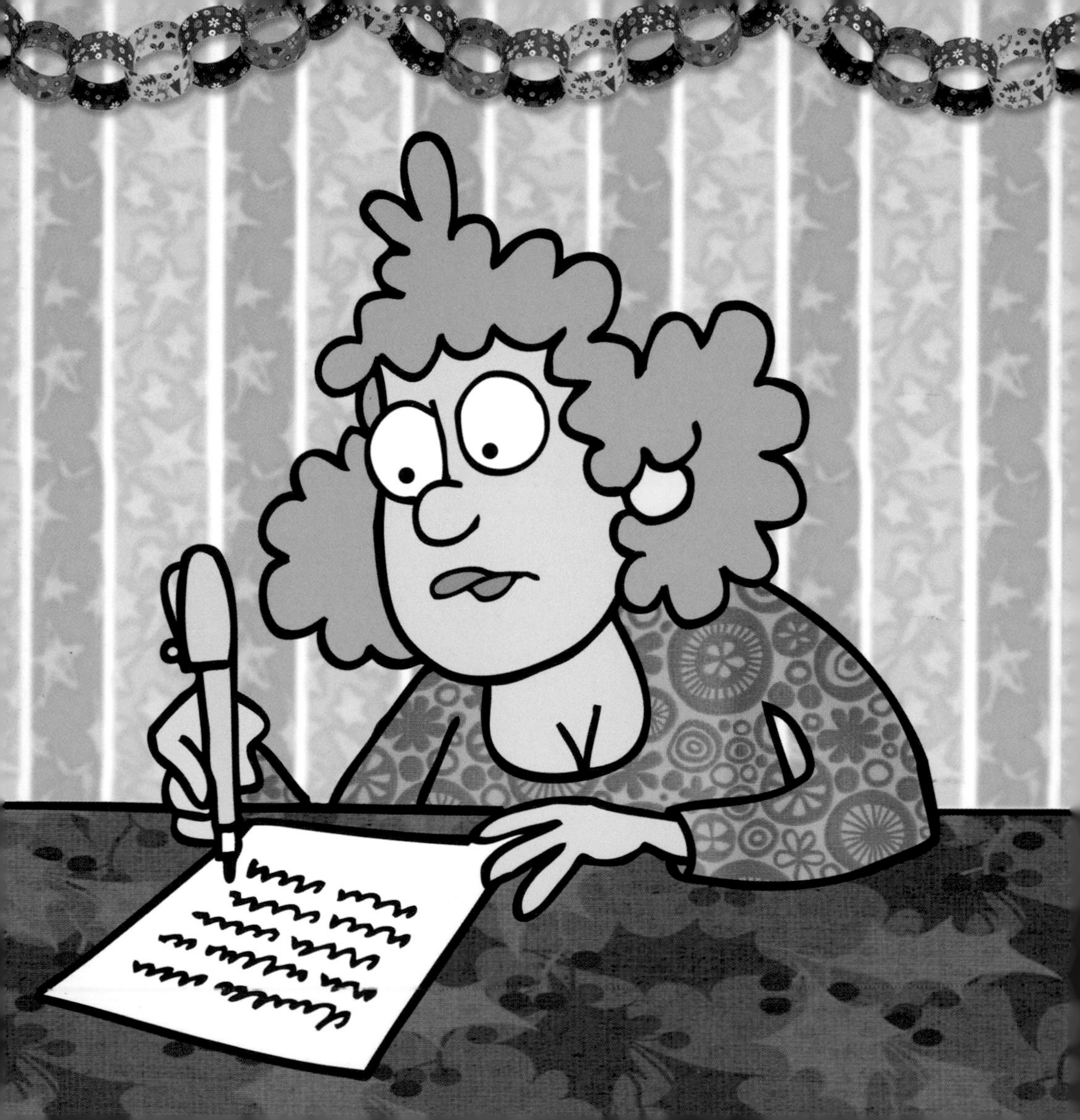

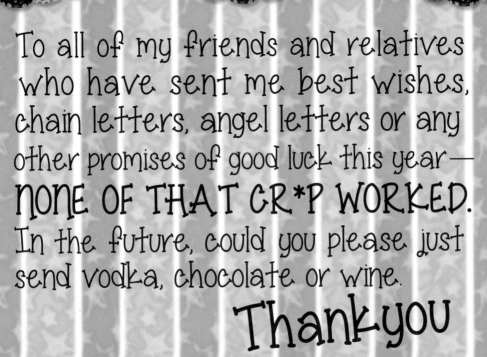

To all of my friends and relatives who have sent me best wishes, chain letters, angel letters or any other promises of good luck this year— NONE OF THAT CR*P WORKED. In the future, could you please just send vodka, chocolate or wine.

Thankyou

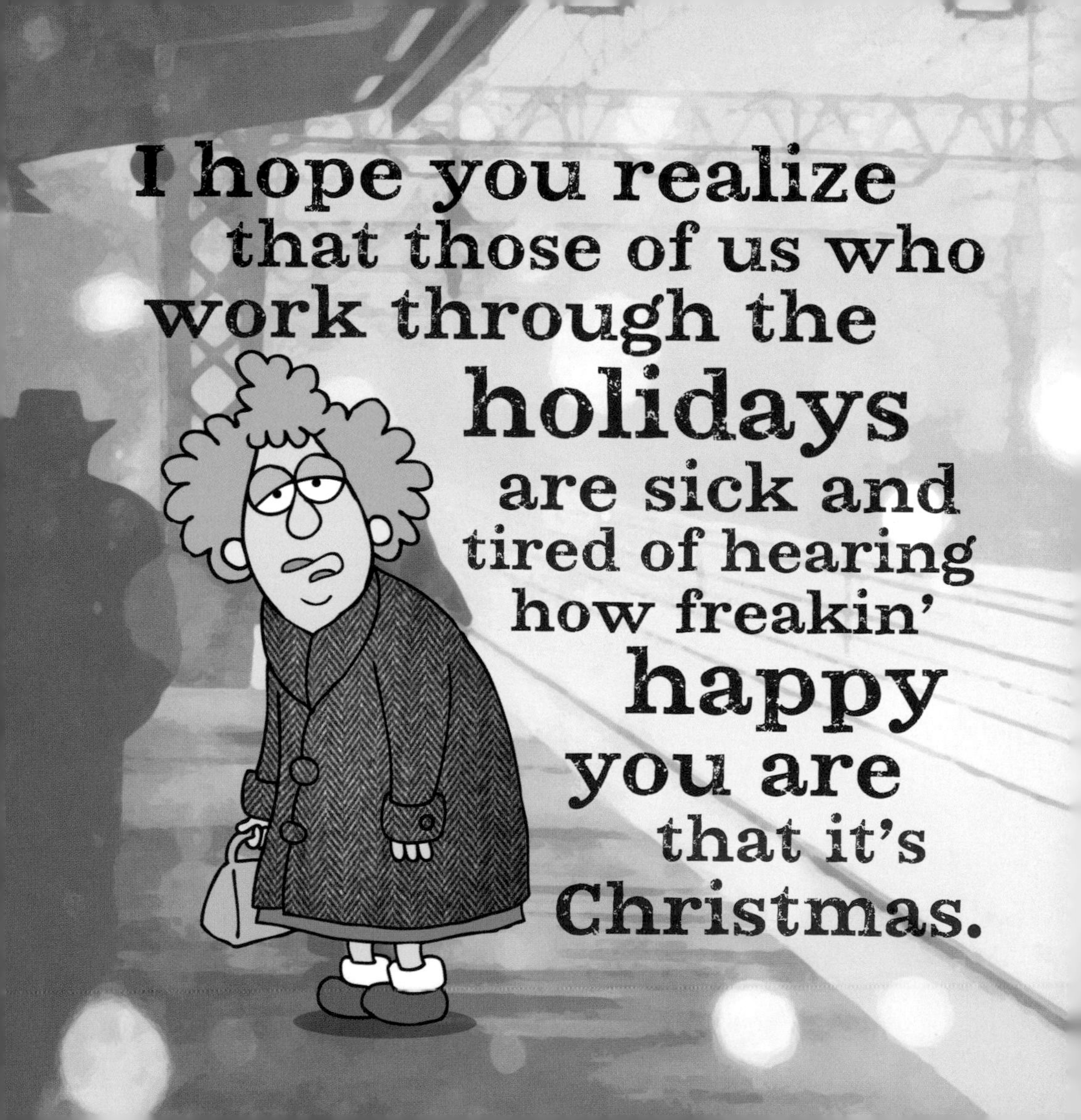
I hope you realize
that those of us who
work through the
holidays
are sick and
tired of hearing
how freakin'
happy
you are
that it's
Christmas.

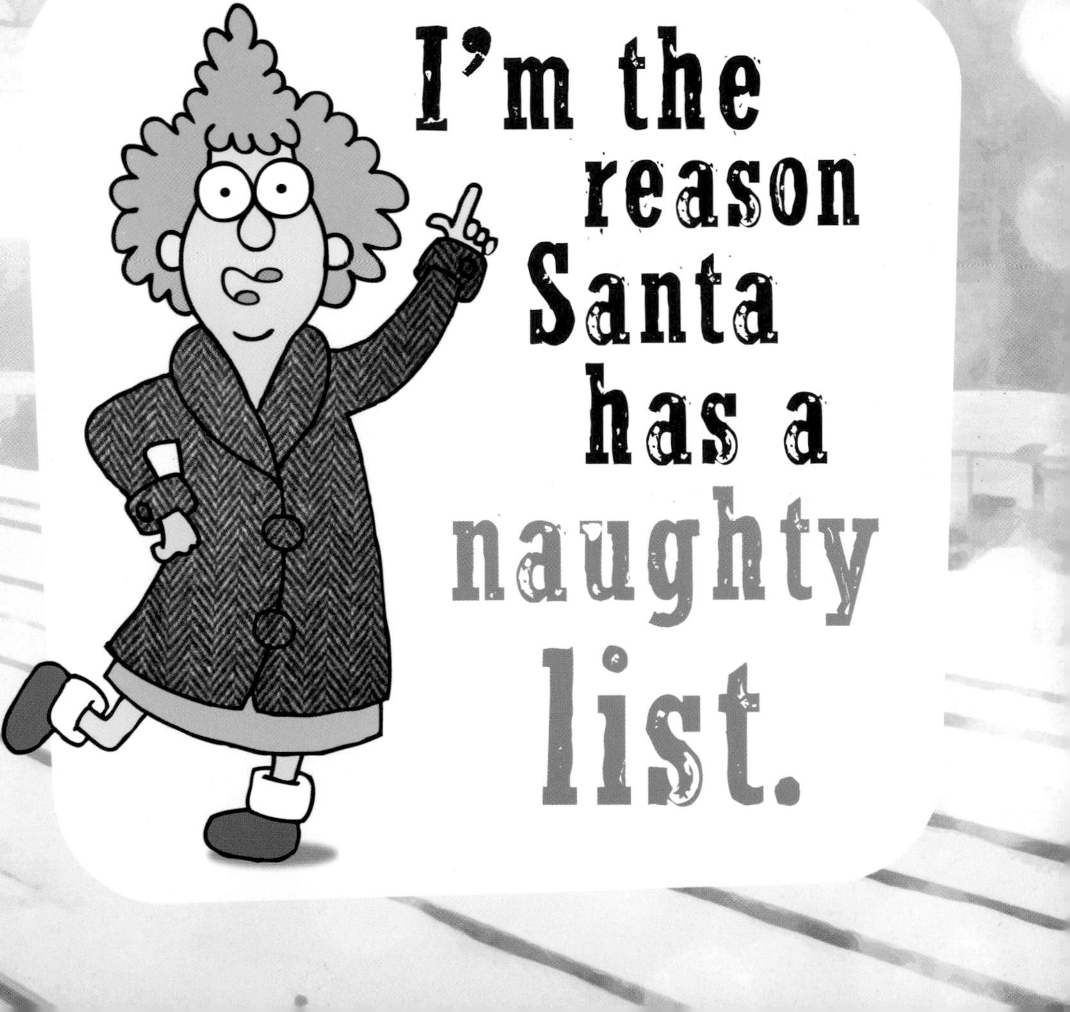

I'm the reason Santa has a naughty list.

I don't seem to have much problem getting **back into shape** after Christmas.

Mind you, it does help when your regular shape is round.

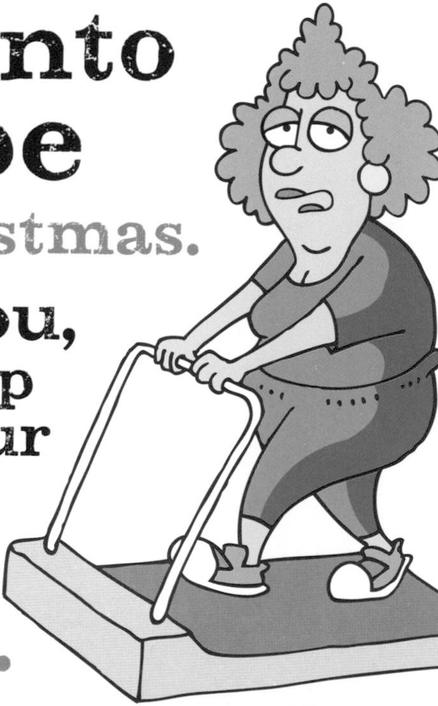

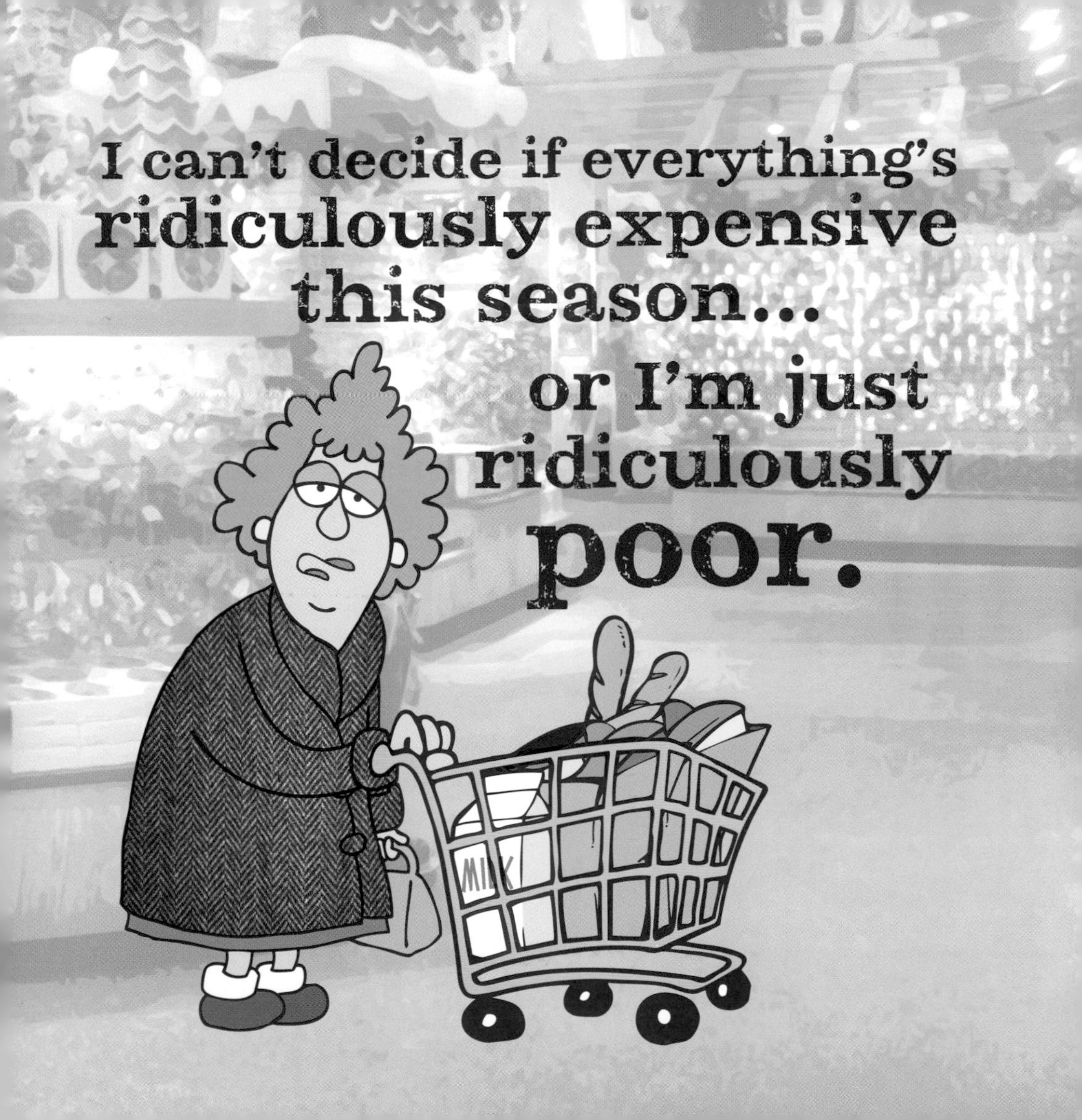
I can't decide if everything's ridiculously expensive this season...
or I'm just ridiculously poor.
MILK

I'm cooking **Christmas dinner for ten...** the guests have usually left by then.

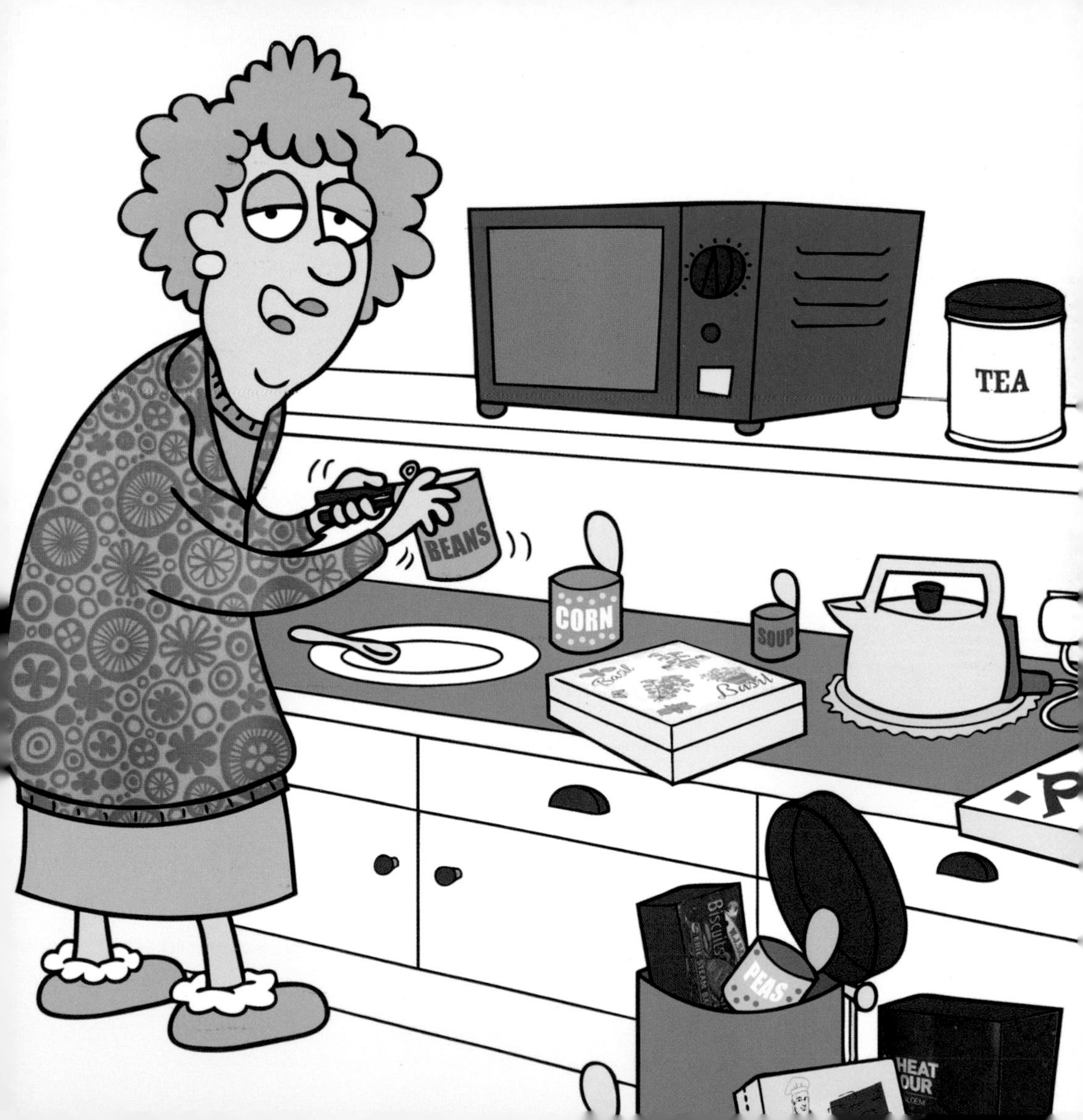
TEA
BEANS
CORN
SOUP
Basil
Basil
PEAS

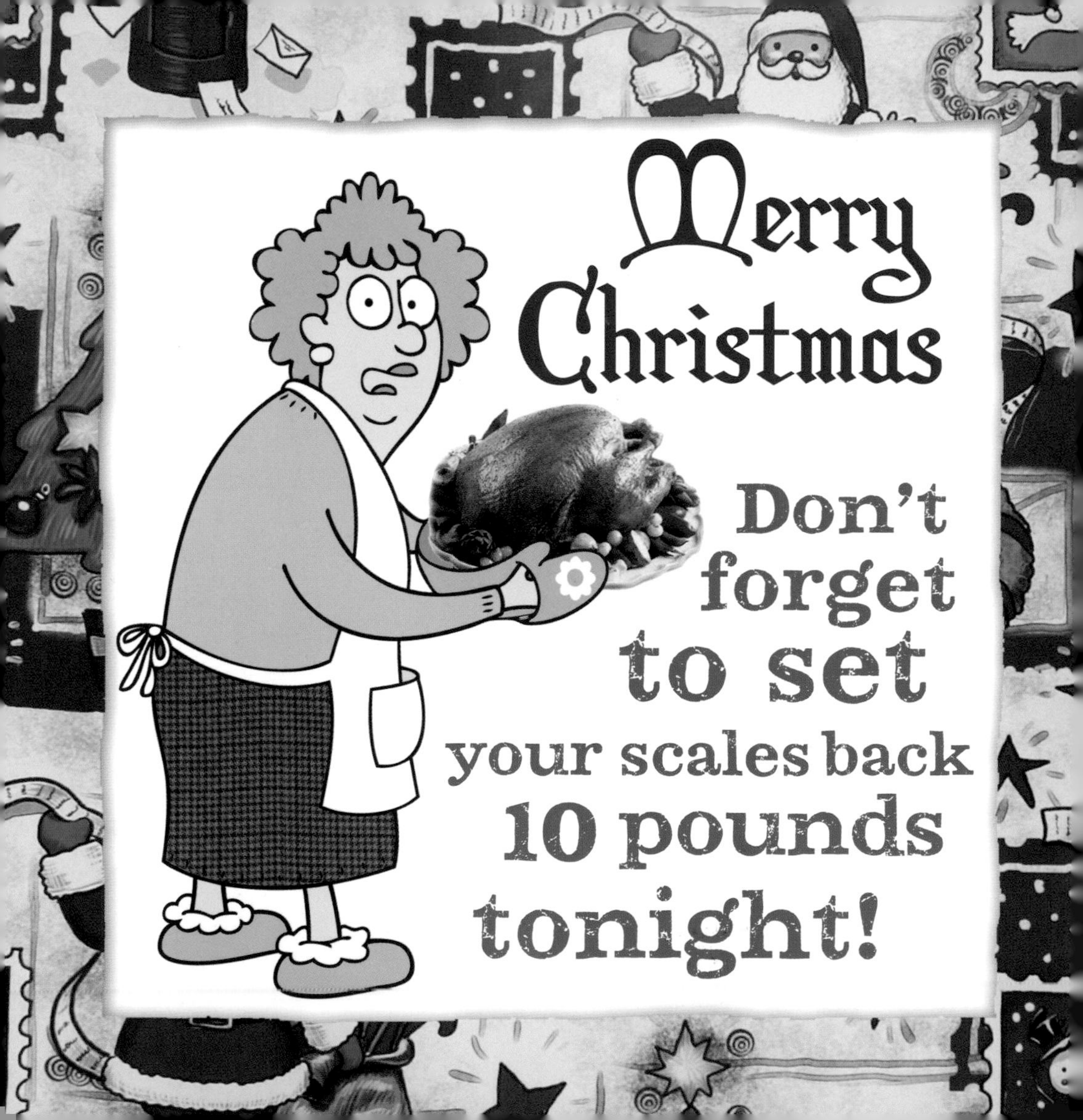
Merry Christmas
Don't forget to set your scales back 10 pounds tonight!

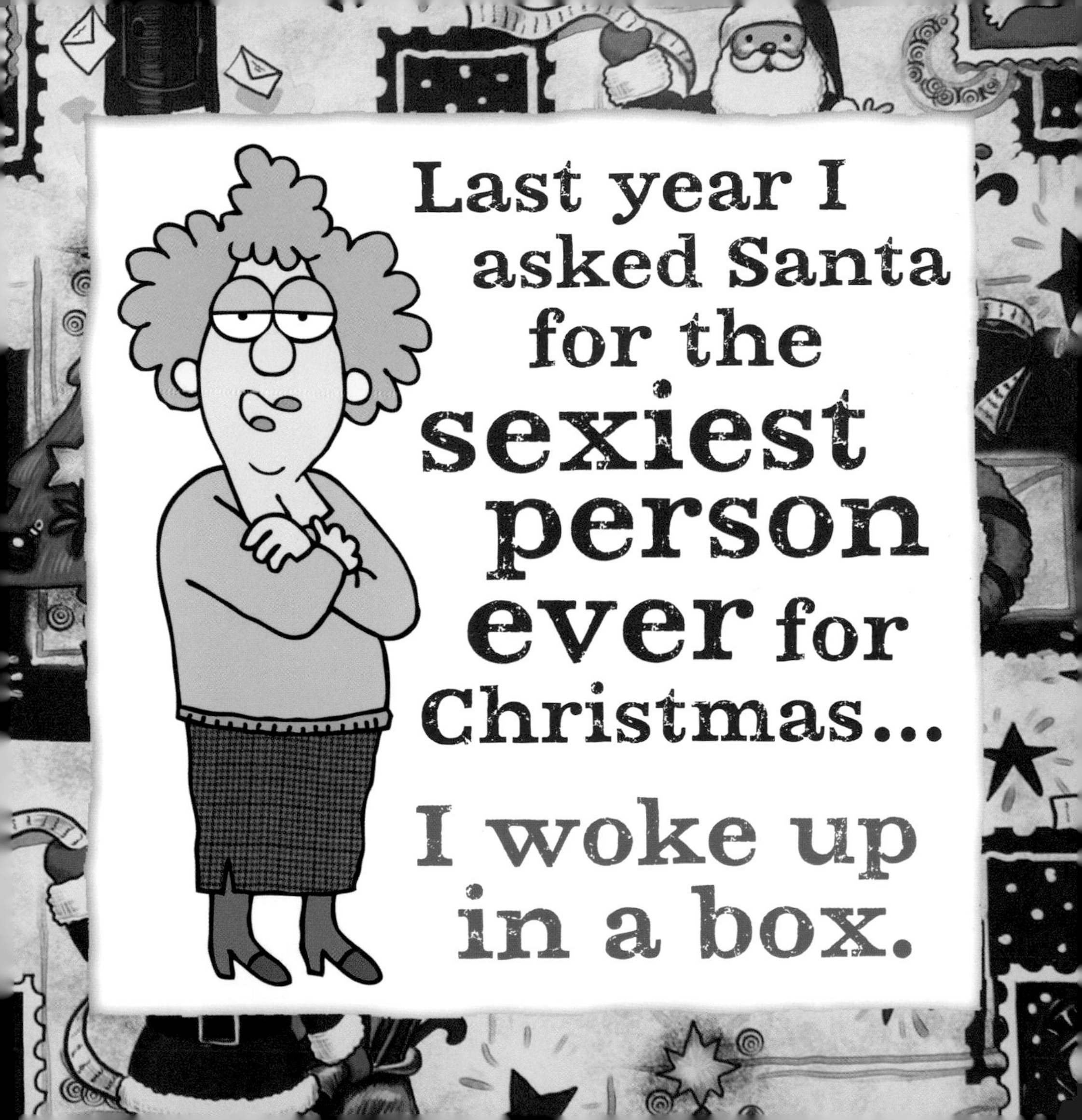
Last year I asked Santa for the sexiest person ever for Christmas...
I woke up in a box.

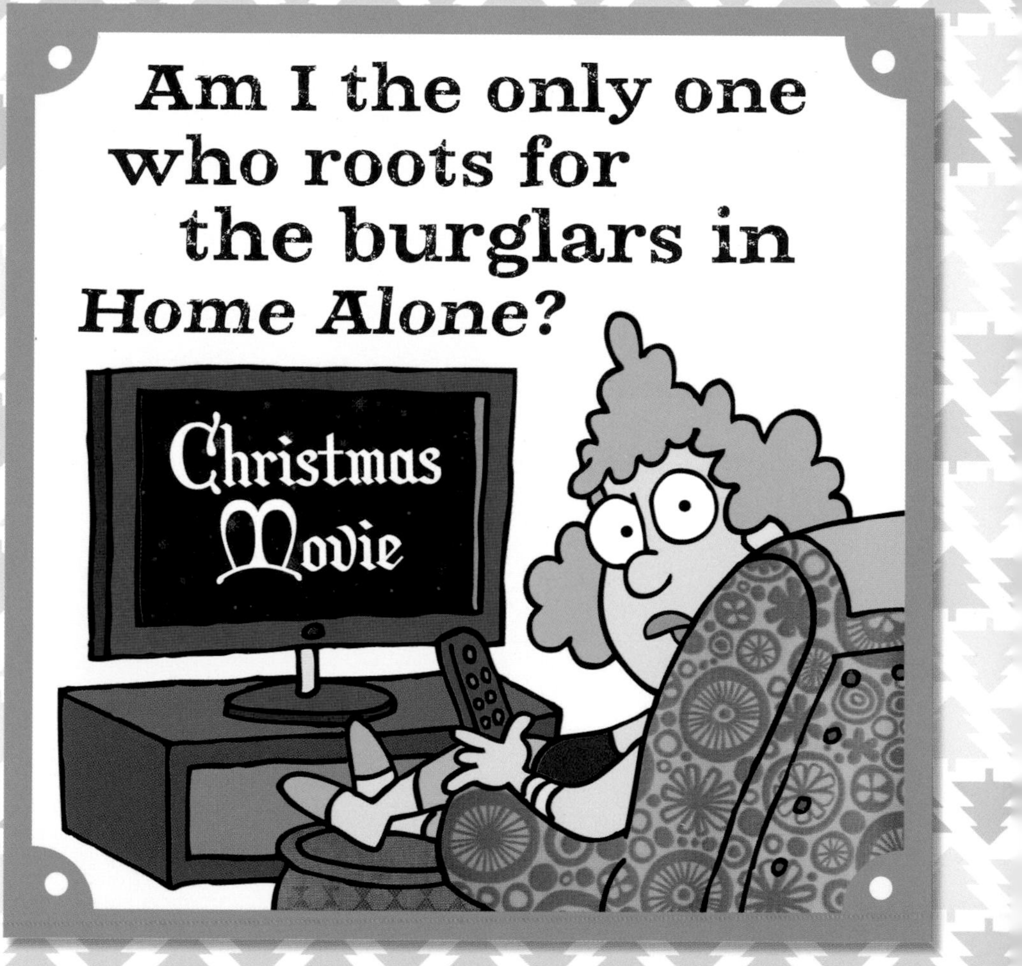

Am I the only one who roots for the burglars in *Home Alone*?
Christmas Movie

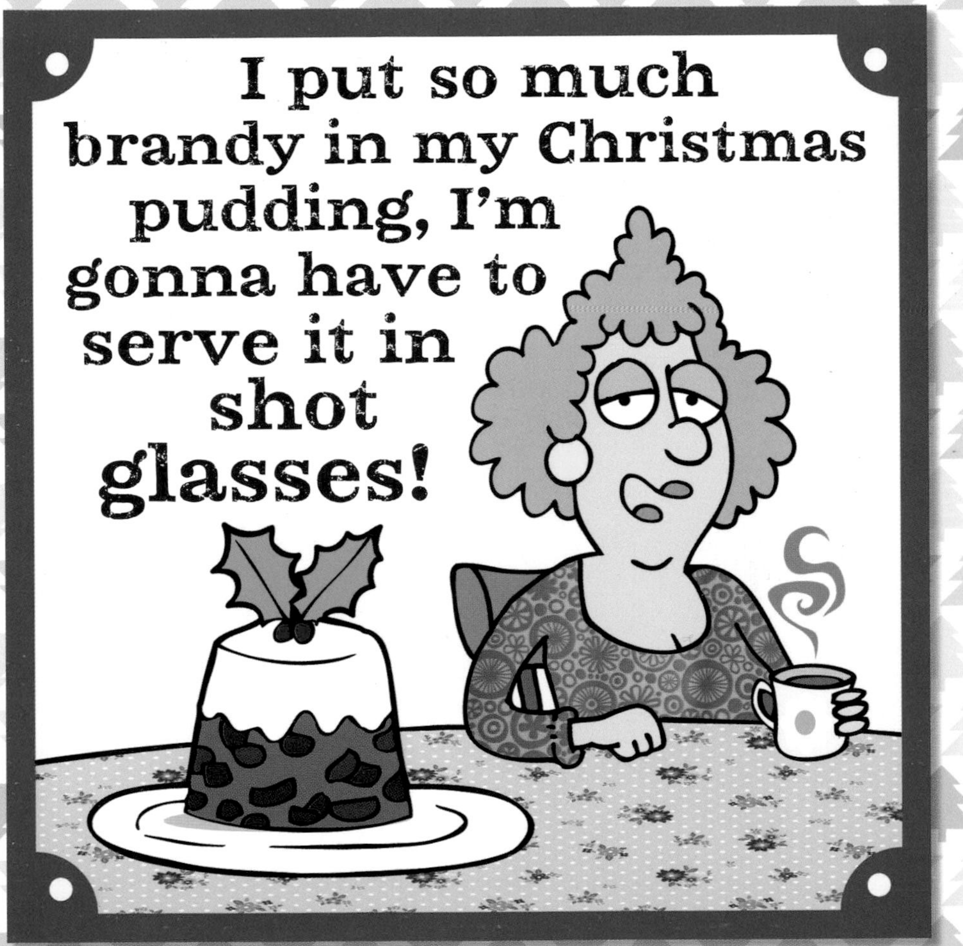
I put so much brandy in my Christmas pudding, I'm gonna have to serve it in shot glasses!

Every Christmas I spend a small fortune on gifts for the grandkids, and every year they've broken them all by **Boxing Day!**

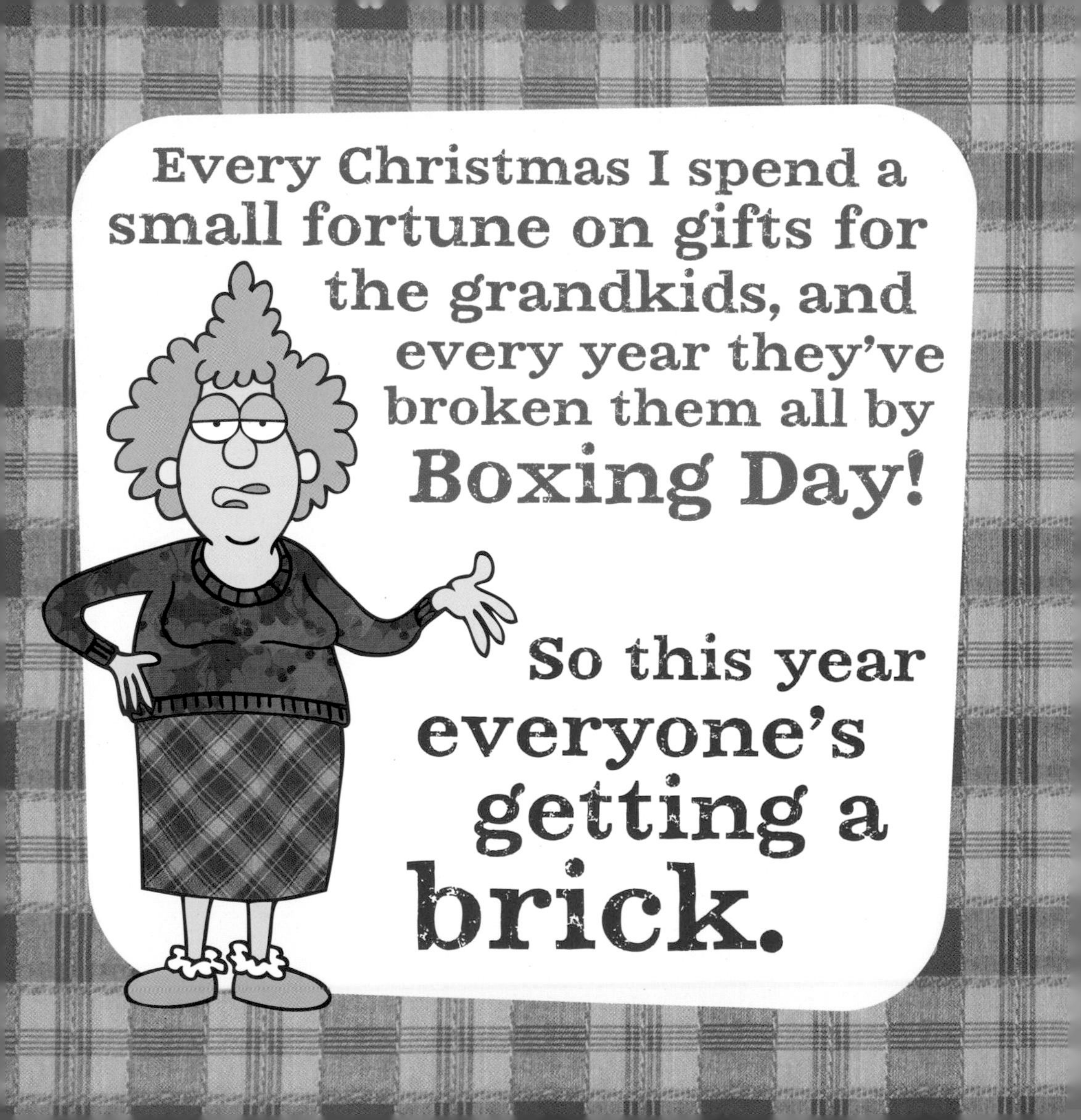

So this year everyone's getting a brick.

WALT'S CHRISTMAS JINGLE

Don't buy me anymore Christmas socks,
I've already got more than I need.
I'm a Christmas grinch this year
Not a freakin' centipede!

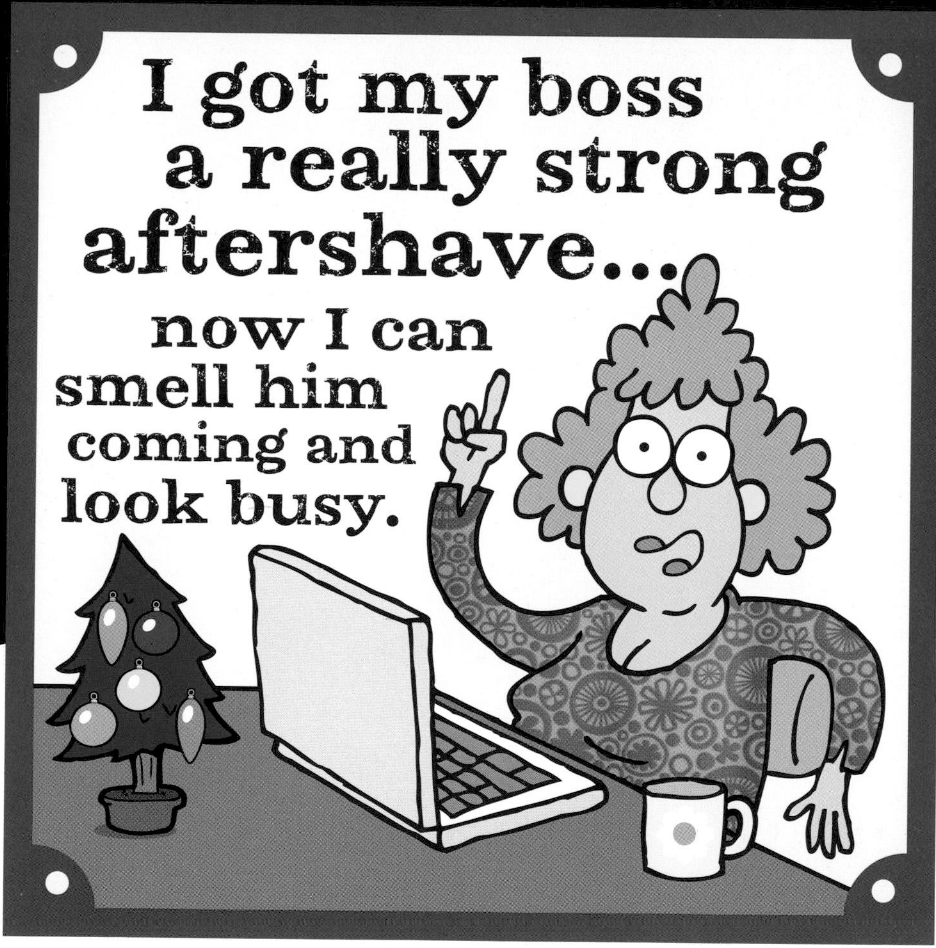
I got my boss a really strong aftershave...
now I can smell him coming and look busy.

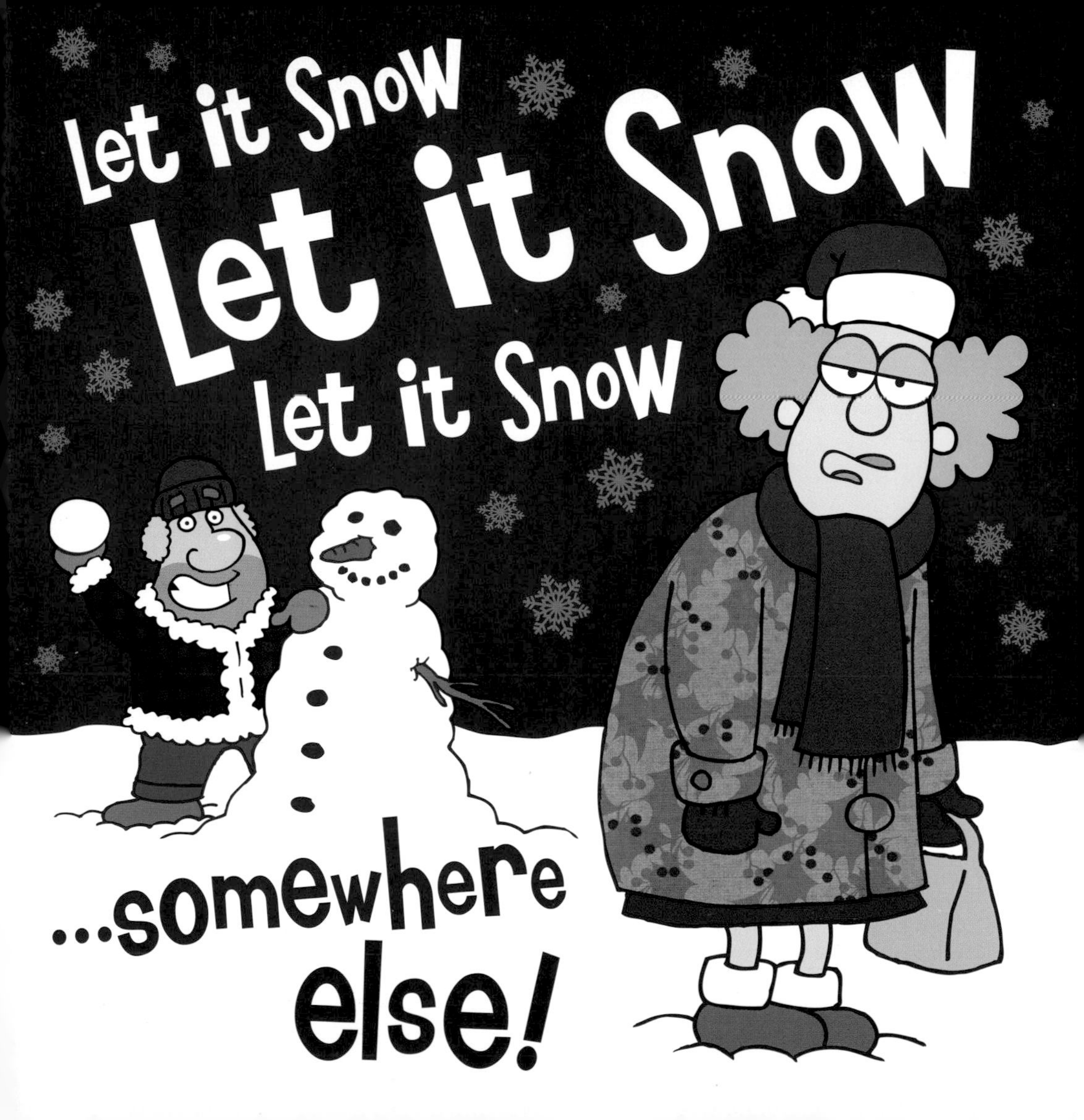
Let it Snow
Let it Snow
Let it Snow
...somewhere else!

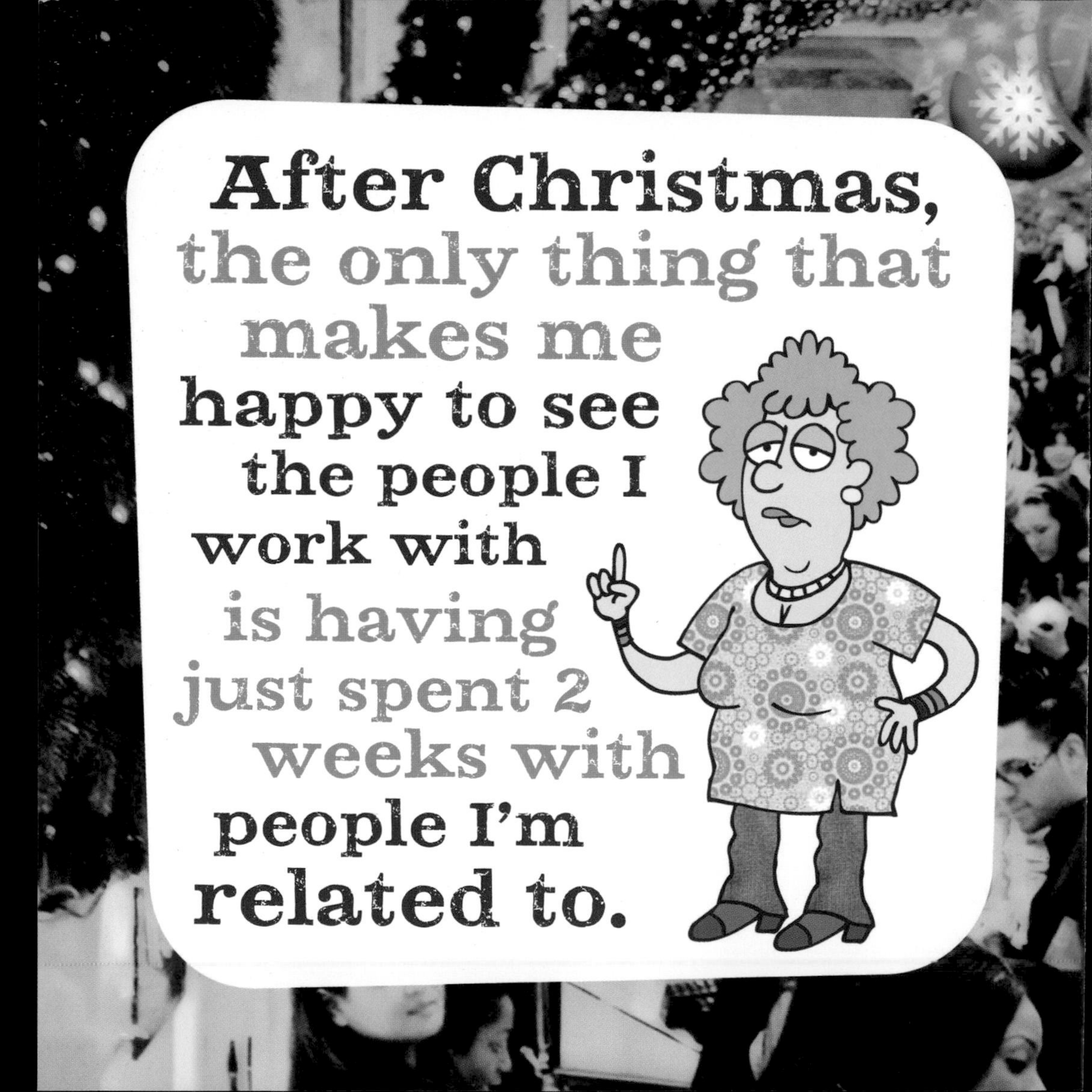
After Christmas, the only thing that makes me happy to see the people I work with is having just spent 2 weeks with people I'm related to.

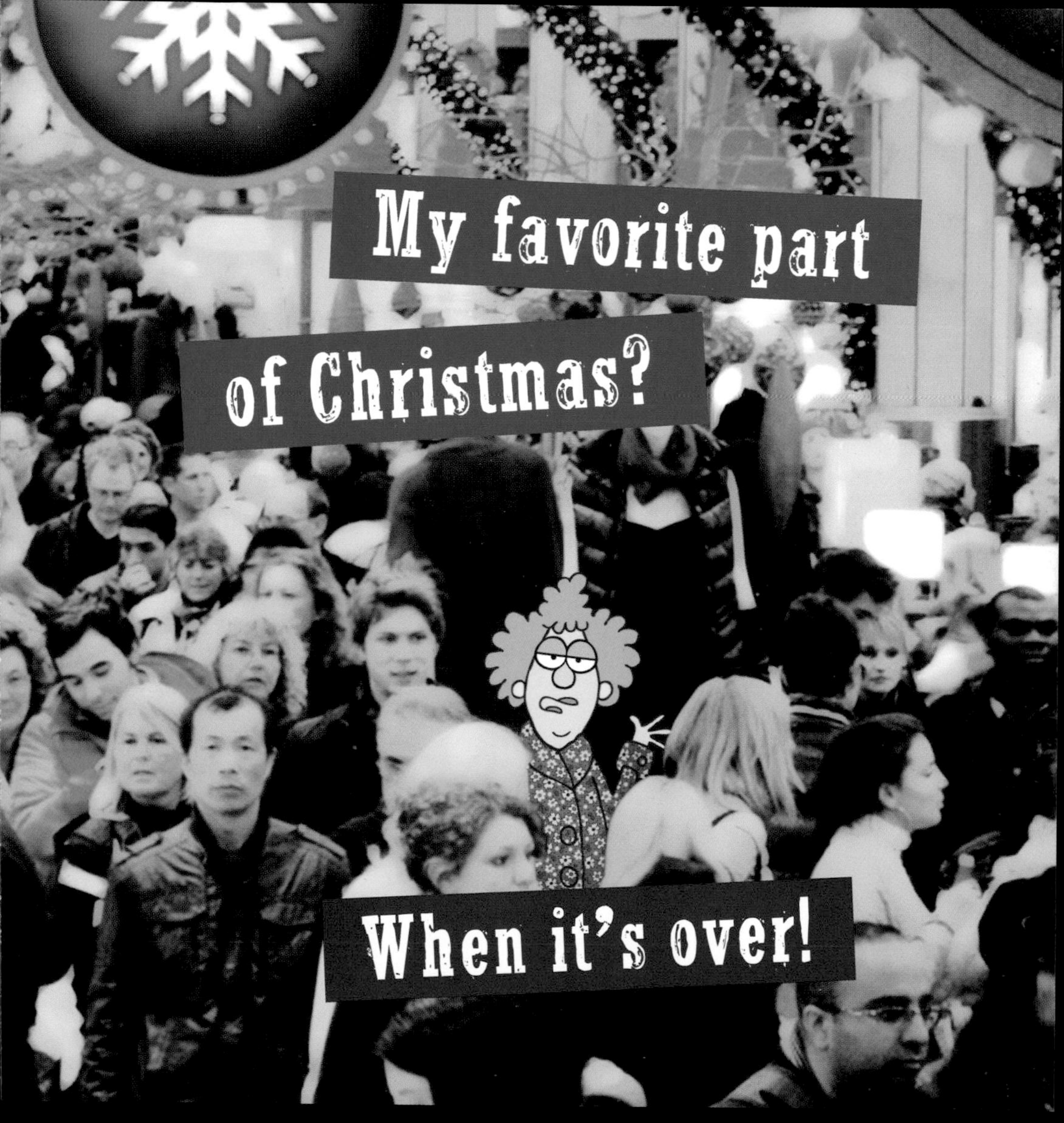
My favorite part
of Christmas?
When it's over!

The Nightmare after Christmas

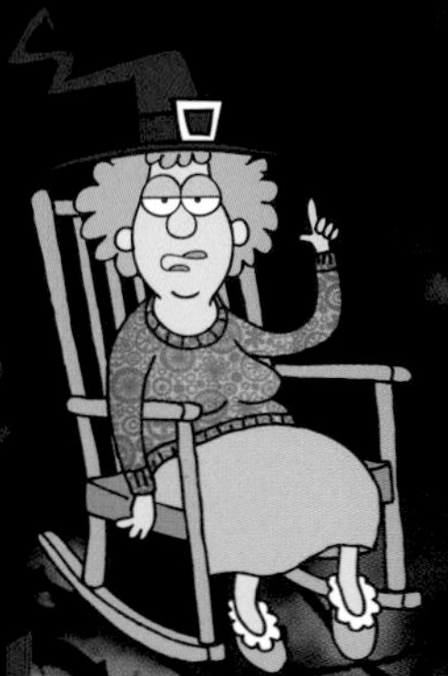

'Twas the month after Christmas and all through the house...

...nothing would fit me,
not even a blouse.
The cookies I'd
nibble,
the eggnog I'd
taste,
all the holiday parties
had gone to my waist....

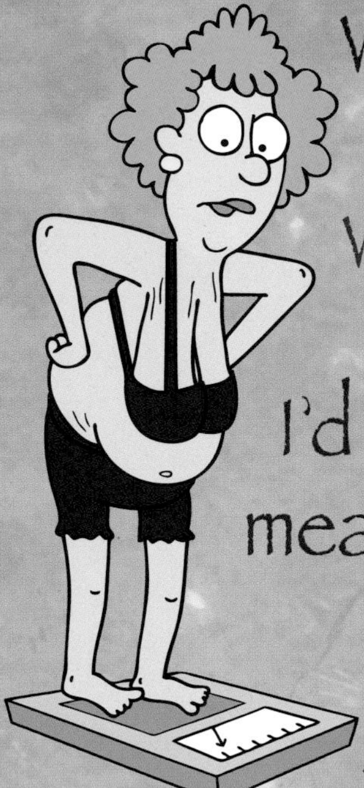

When I got on the scales,
there arose such a number!
When I walked to the store
(less a walk than a lumber),
I'd remember the marvelous
meals I'd prepared –
the gravies
and sauces
and beef
nicely rared,

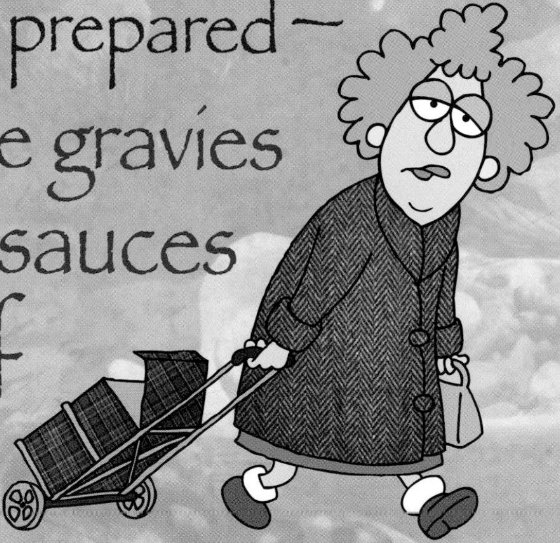

the wine and the rum balls,

the bread

and the cheese –

and the way I'd never said,

"No thank *you*,

please."

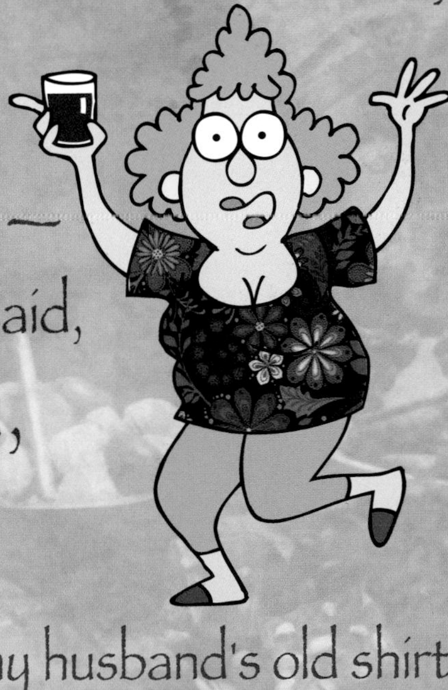

As I dressed myself in my husband's old shirt

and prepared once again

to do battle with dirt…

I said to myself, as I only can,
"You can't spend the winter
disguised as a man!"

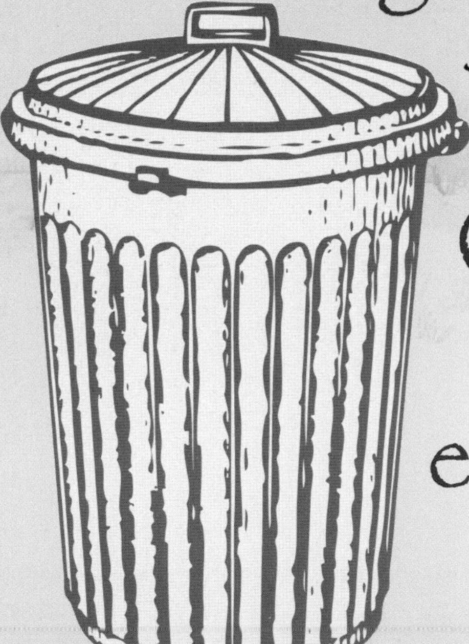

So, away with the last
of the sour cream dip.
Get rid of
the fruit cake,
each cracker
and chip.

Every last bit of food
that I like must be banished
'til all the additional
ounces have
vanished.

I won't have a cookie,

not even a lick.

I want only to chew

on a celery stick....

I won't have hot biscuits,
or corn bread, or pie;
I'll munch on a carrot
and quietly cry.
I'm hungry, I'm lonesome
and life is a bore.
But isn't that what
January
is for?

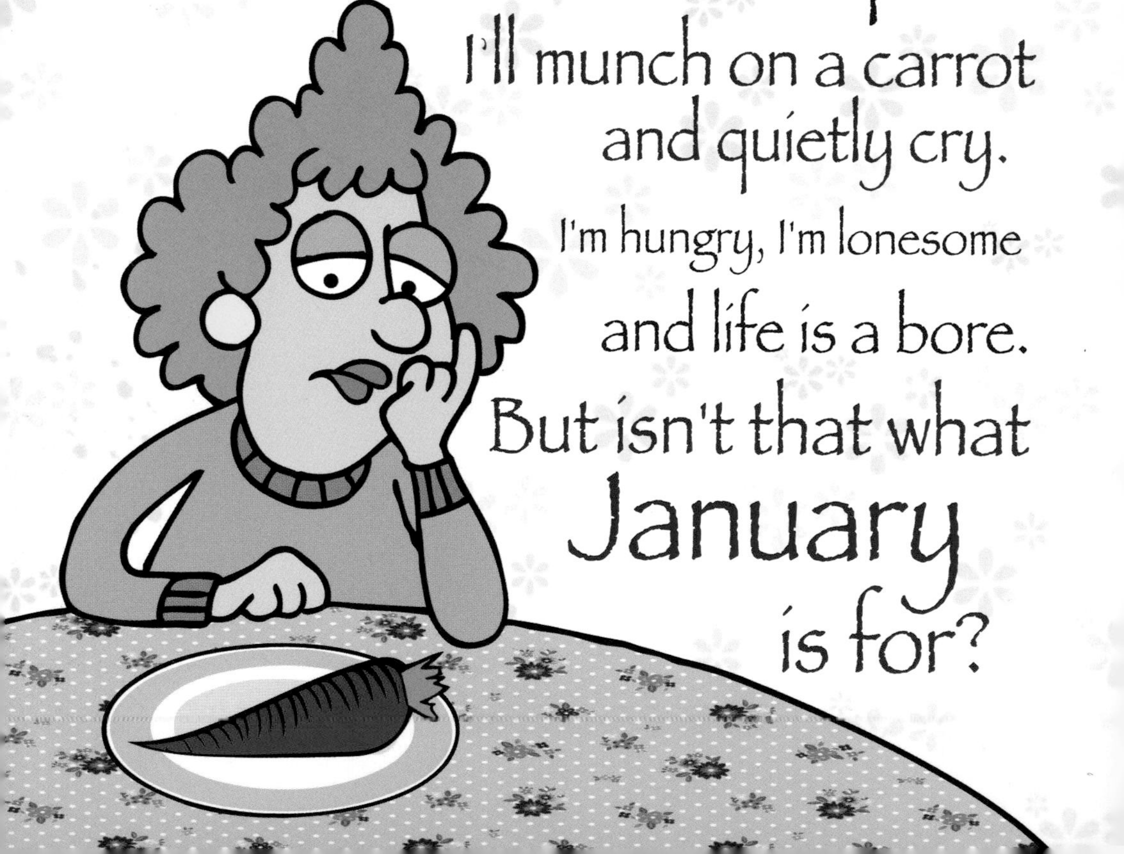

Unable to

giggle,

no longer

a riot.

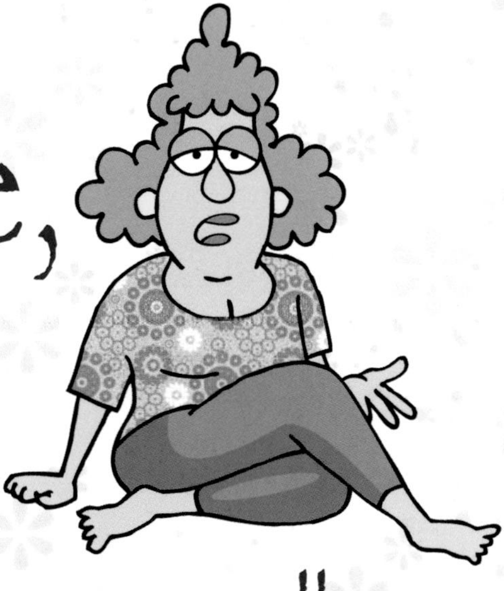

Happy New Year to all

and to all a good

DIET!

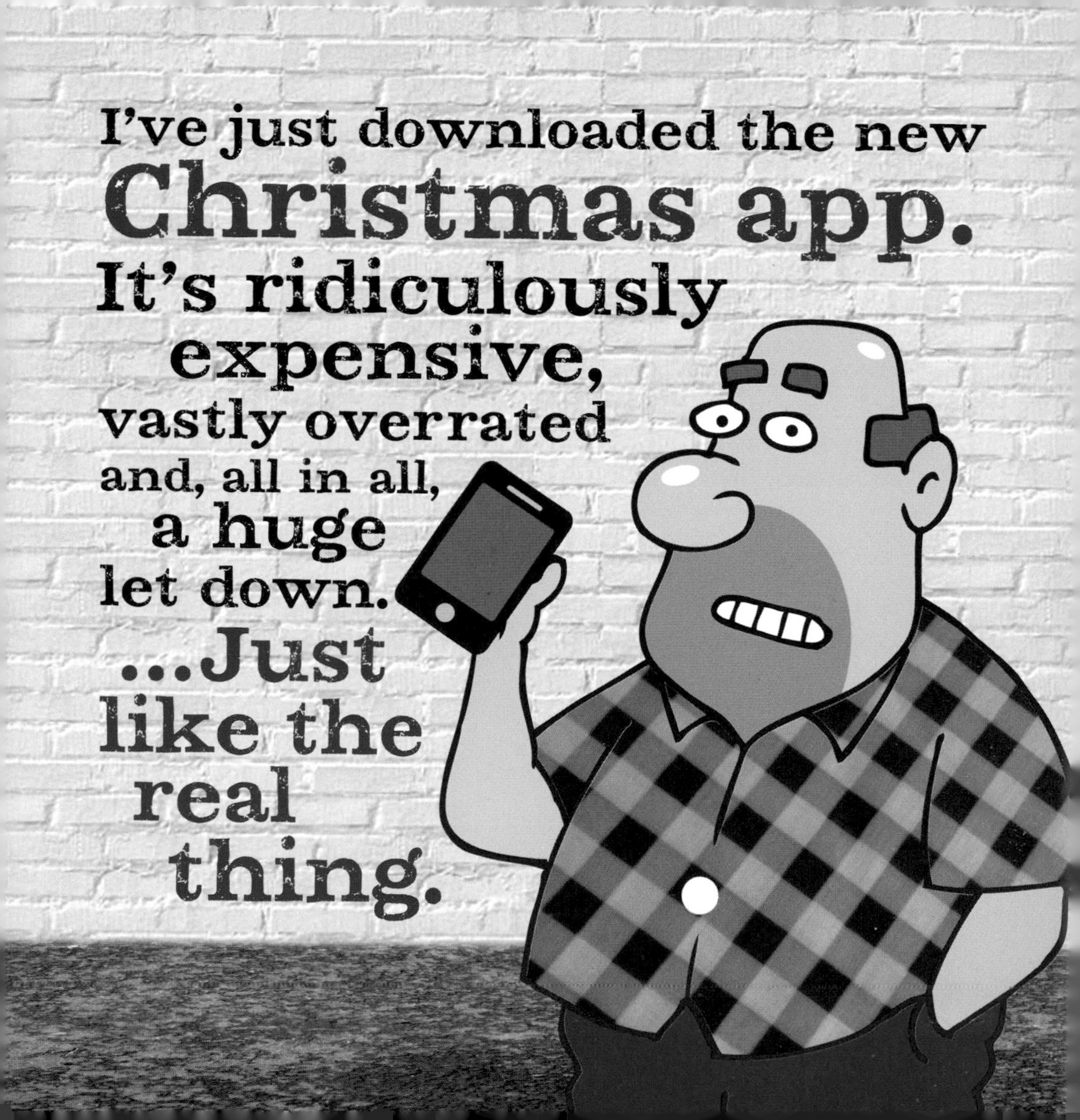
I've just downloaded the new
Christmas app.
It's ridiculously
expensive,
vastly overrated
and, all in all,
a huge
let down.
...Just
like the
real
thing.

I always say the best way to survive Christmas is to take it one panic attack at a time.

I'm serving a seven-course Christmas dinner...

turkey
pizza
and a
six-pack!

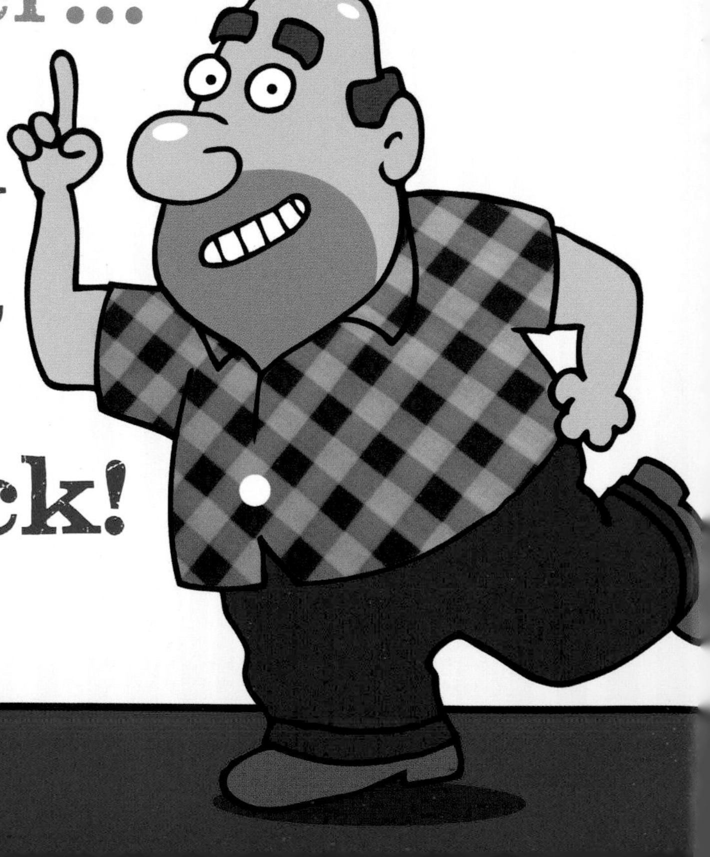

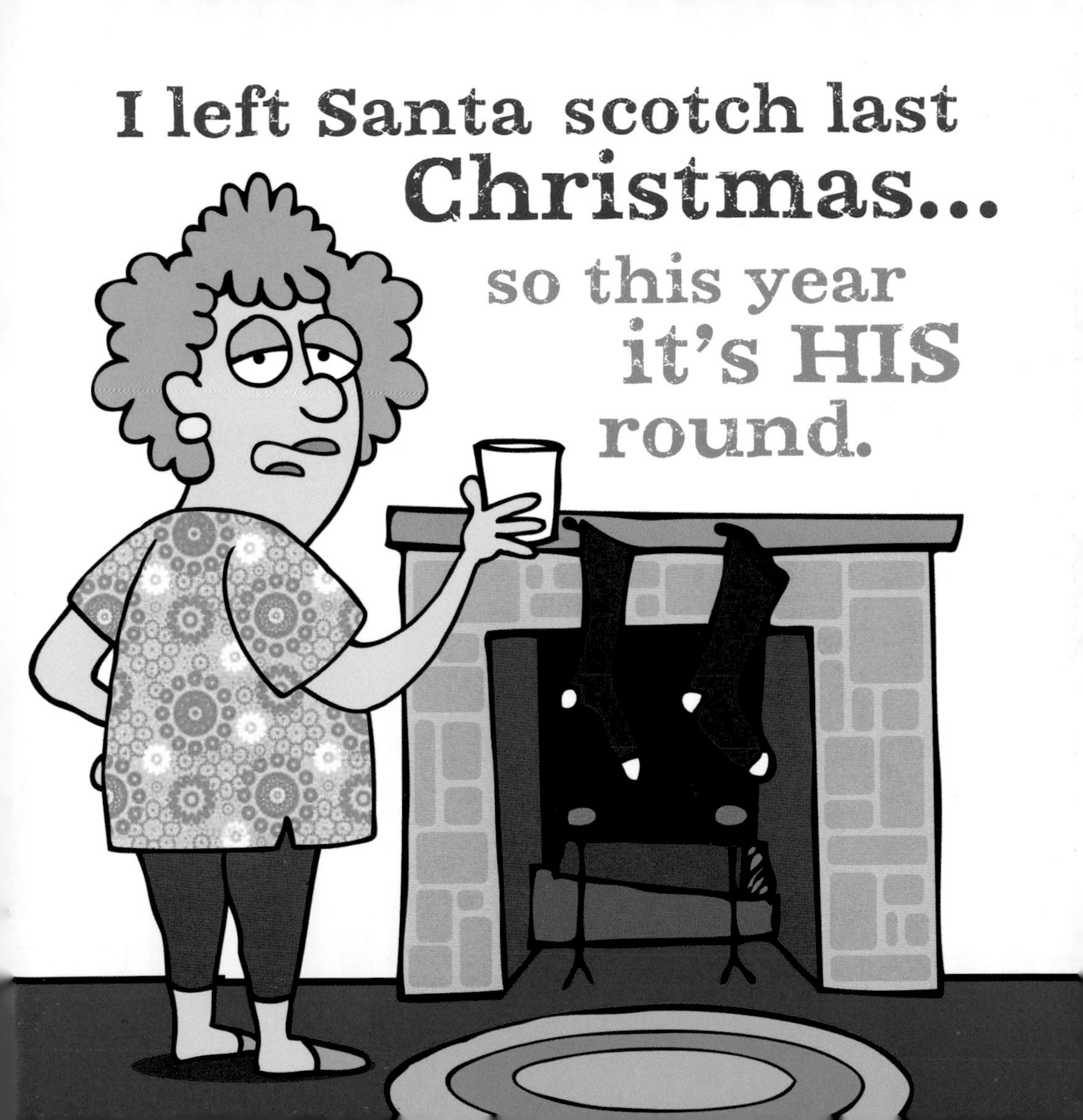
I left Santa scotch last
Christmas...
so this year
it's HIS
round.

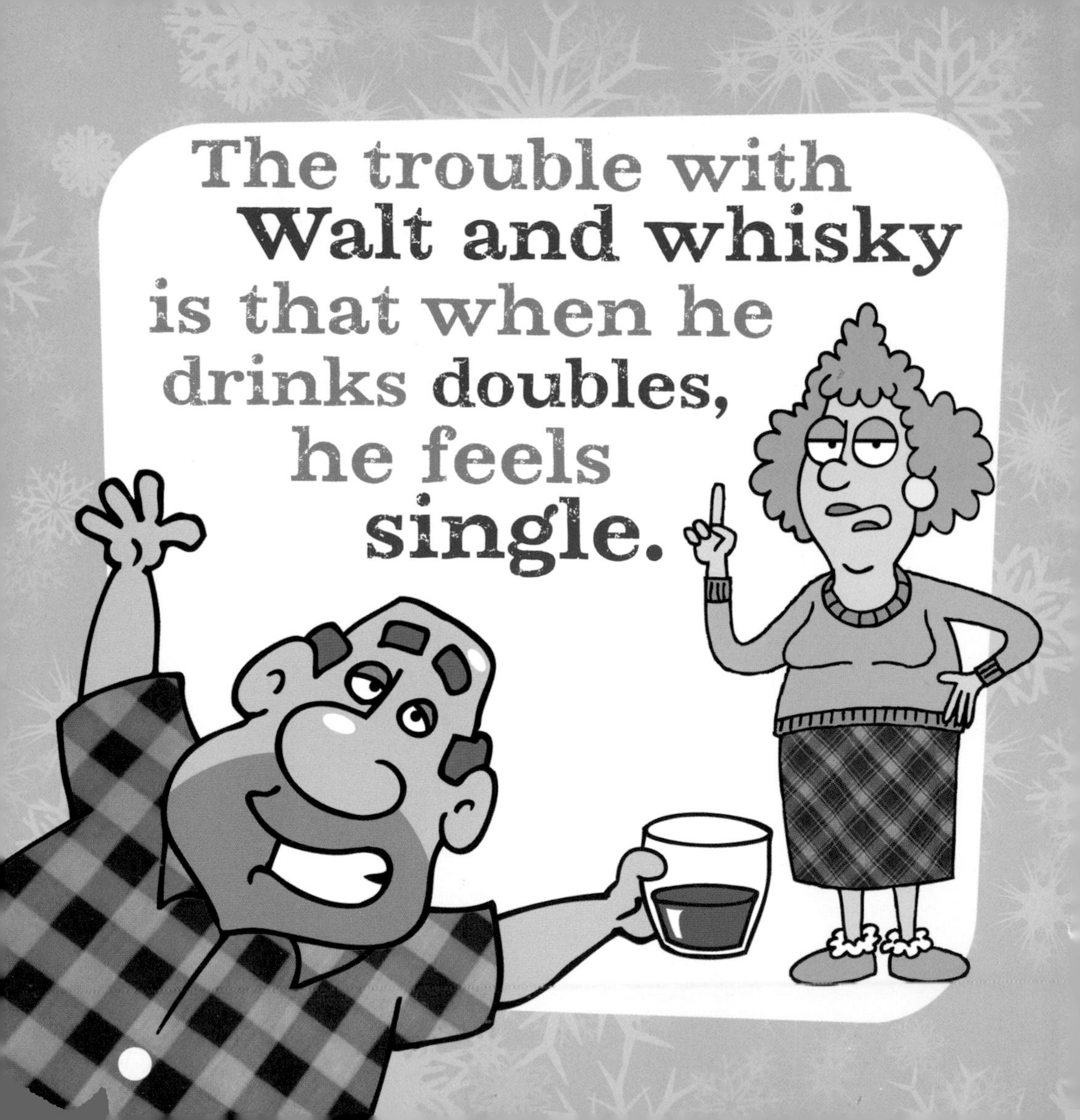
The trouble with
Walt and whisky
is that when he
drinks doubles,
he feels
single.

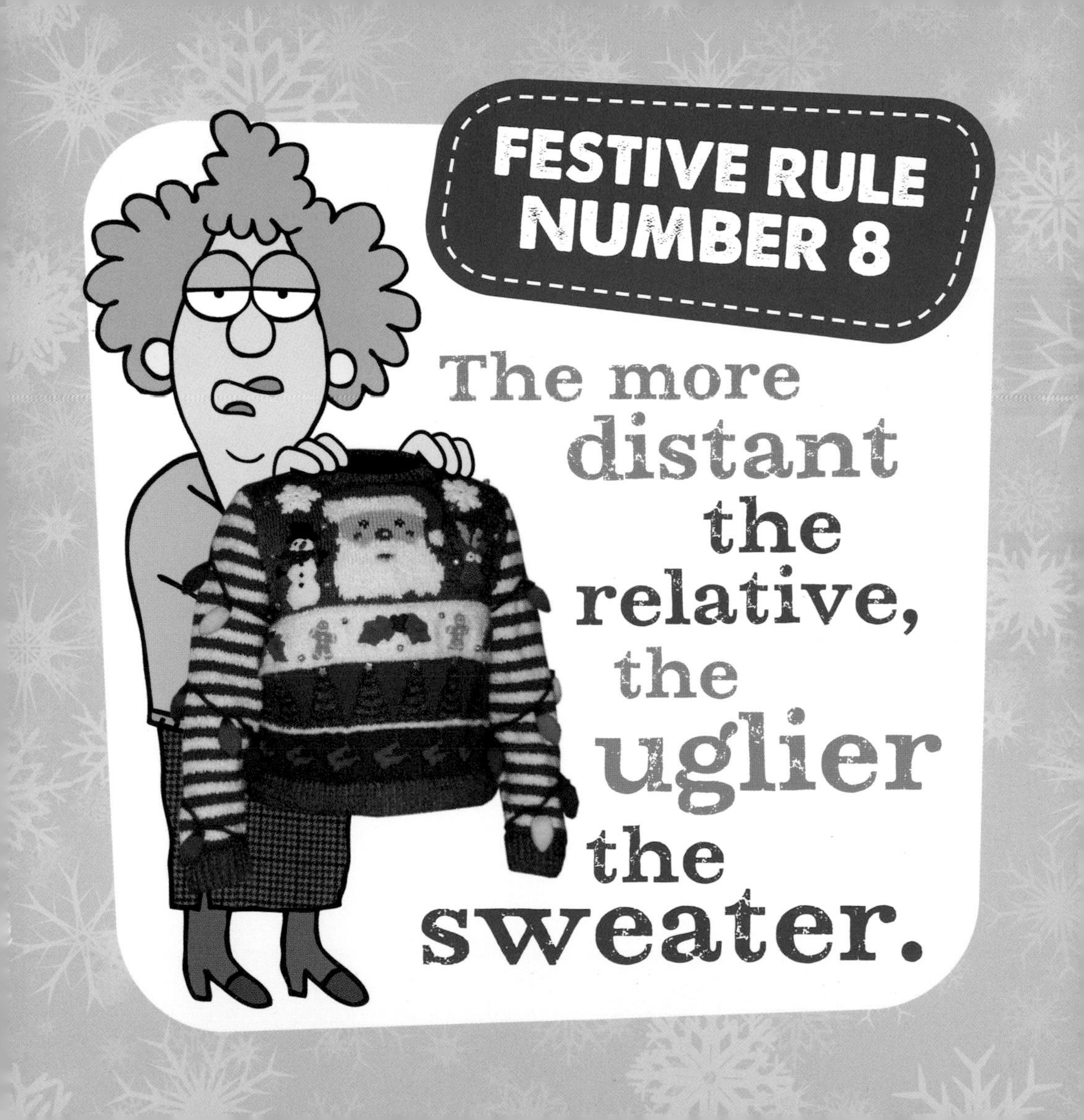

FESTIVE RULE NUMBER 8

The more distant the relative, the uglier the sweater.

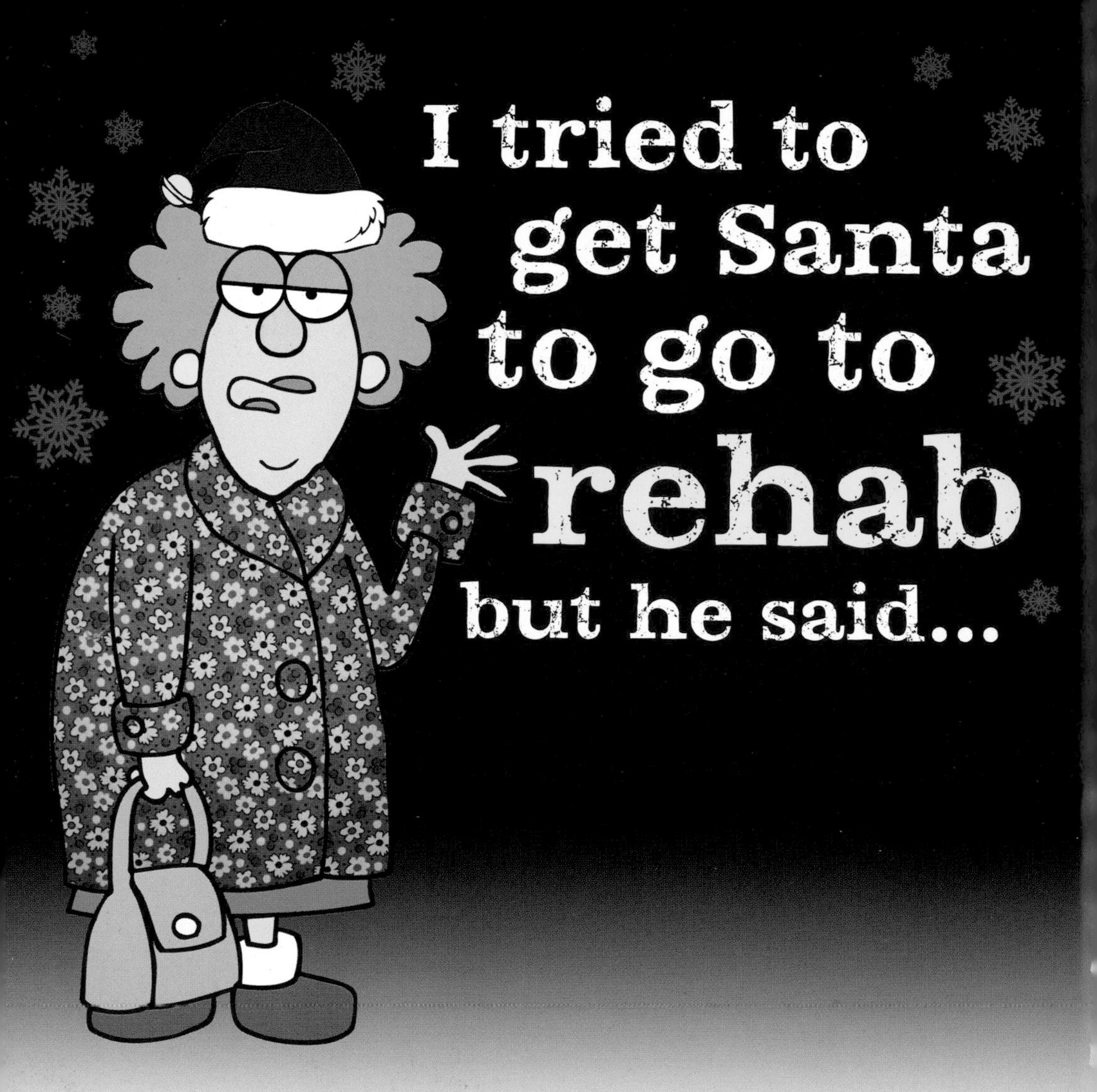

I tried to get Santa to go to rehab but he said...

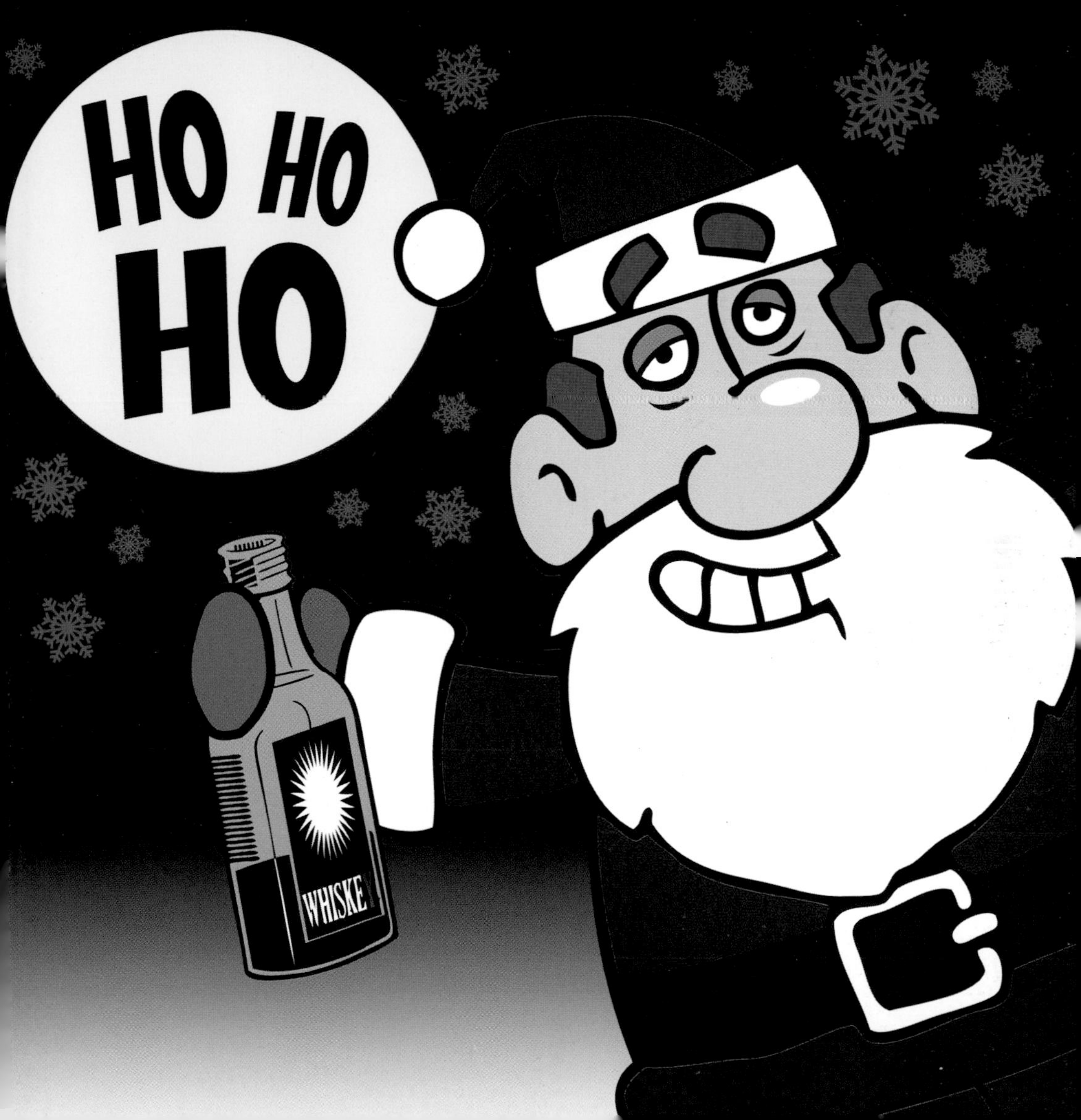
HO HO HO
WHISKEY

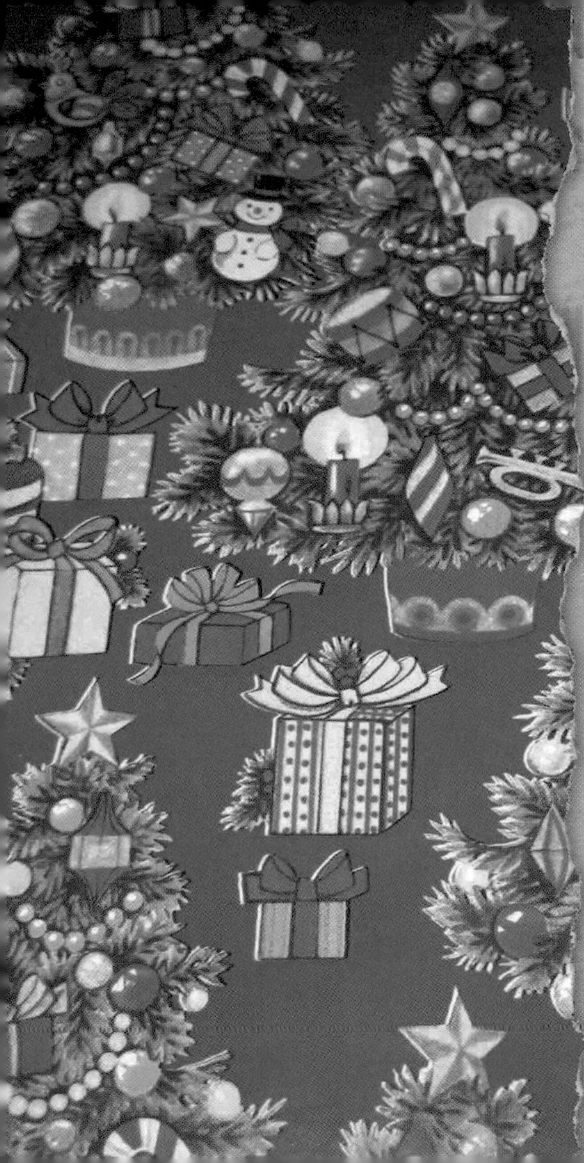

First Edition
18 17 16 15 14 5 4 3 2 1

Published by
Gibbs Smith
P.O. Box 667
Layton, Utah 84041

1.800.835.4993 orders
www.gibbs-smith.com

Illustrations by
Dave Iddon @ The Backland Studio
Designed by Dave Iddon
Contributed material by
Raychel Backland

Printed and bound in China

Gibbs Smith books are printed on either recycled, 100% post-consumer waste, FSC-certified papers or on paper produced from sustainable PEFC-certified forest/controlled wood source. Learn more at www.pefc.org.

ISBN 13: 978-1-4236-3763-9

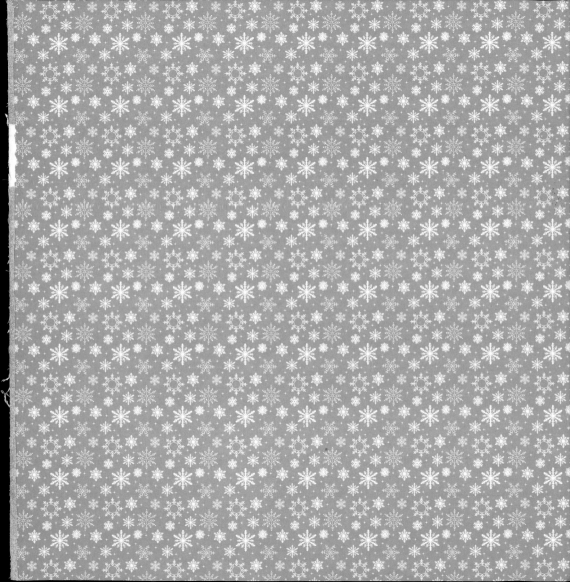